101 Stupid Things Trainers Do To Sabotage Success

Nancy Stern

Maggi Payment

Richard Chang Associates, Inc.
Publications Division
Irvine, California

101 Stupid Things Trainers Do To Sabotage Success

Nancy Stern
Maggi Payment

Library of Congress Catalog Card Number
95-68866

ISBN 1-883553-93-8

Editor:	Sarah Ortlieb Fraser
Graphic Layout:	Christina Slater
Cover Design:	John Odam, Eric Strand, and Christina Slater

Sixth Printing February 1999

Richard Chang Associates, Inc., Publications Division
15265 Alton Parkway, Suite 300
Irvine, CA 92618
(800) 756-8096   (949) 727-7477
Fax (949) 727-7007
www.richardchangassociates.com

About The Authors

Nancy Stern, M.A., is President of Communication Plus, a management and employee development firm in Del Mar, California, which specializes in providing holistic communication skills training, education and consulting. She is a columnist and an EMMY award-winner, appearing in her own nationally syndicated PBS television series. Since 1972 she has been presenting hundreds of workshops and seminars throughout the U.S. and Canada.

Maggi Payment, M.Ed., is Director of the Center For Worktime Options in San Diego, California, a training and consulting firm specializing in employee and organization development with an emphasis on flexible work arrangements. During the past twenty years she has written numerous feature articles for national publications and has conducted hundreds of workshops and seminars in the U.S. and Canada.

Acknowledgments

As training professionals, we have all experienced stupid things. This book would not have been possible had it not been for the creative input from our colleagues. We express our gratitude to Joel Hochberger, Doug Sjoberg, Dallas Strawn, Julie Mazo, Kevan Schlamowitz, Gary Corwin, Trudy Nelson, Nancy Gorski, Kathleen Latham, Steve Anderman, K.C. Brady, Doug Gross, Rickie Hall, Jo Schaefer, Lisa Reynolds, Keith Kelly, Dan Schulte, Cathy Bolger, Janis Whitaker, Lisa Newman, Louis Spain, Christine Bevel, Joe Warden, and Richard Baudrand.

We also thank all the audiences we have been blessed to educate not only for their inspiration, but also for educating us.

Table of Contents

3. Things You Say Or Hear 31

Introduction

"It's the little details that make a big difference"

Stern & Payment

Trainers are often called presenters, facilitators, speakers, or educators. They are never called boring, insensitive, careless, or unimaginative. Or, are they?

When forced to confess, most trainers admit stories about stupid things they have done while developing and delivering programs to teach workplace skills and information. Is it necessary to learn the hard way, one stupid thing at a time? Must we make a lot of stupid mistakes, live with the memories, and plod on?

Not necessarily. We can identify stupid things to avoid in the first place, and learn how to avoid them.

Better Late Than Never

Successful trainers have something in common with professional ice skaters, dancers, bowlers, and golfers. Professionals make what they do look so effortless we all think we can easily do it too. Then we discover it isn't so.

To become good at what we do, we must practice. And practice, and practice. We must continuously improve on all the small details. It's never too late to start.

Can we learn from the mistakes of others? Sure! We asked experienced trainers about their mistakes, and for their advice, so we can all learn from them. If you want to improve all those little details to become a successful professional, this book will help you do that.

You will learn new techniques and strategies, find reminders about best training practices, and begin to improve the small details of your work. And, you can laugh while you learn.

What, Me Too?

Adult educators who are involved in planning, designing, and delivering educational programs and in making continuous improvement will find strategies for successful training. Among those who will find this most useful are:

♦ new trainers

♦ trainer wannabes

♦ experienced trainers

♦ trainers who train other trainers

♦ trainers employed within organizations

♦ external trainers who come into organizations

♦ technical specialists who must provide training

♦ managers or supervisors responsible for training

♦ and yes, that means you too!

Next Time

When you are training to provide knowledge, to build skills, or to change attitudes, this book helps you focus on success strategies. It is a reference tool designed for browsing.

This book is also helpful for training novice trainers. And, it is a useful gift for an experienced trainer.

Professionals work long and hard at every tiny detail to improve what they do, and with this book you can too. You can avoid making the stupid mistakes that separate the novices from the professionals.

Chapter 1

Places You Go

#1 On-Site? Off-Site?

To go off-site or to stay on-site, that is the question. Certain programs are best done off-site, but wind up on-site.

What's Wrong?

 There are too many interruptions with on-site programs.

 Participants are tempted to go back to their desks during breaks, and they lose program focus.

 People who return to their desks return late to the class.

 People who return to their desks may stay there.

RING!

Some Success Strategies:

Go off-site whenever possible, remembering to plan for money in the budget for off-site expenses. When on-site, beg people not to return to their desks. Also, put a note on the door that says ENTER AT YOUR OWN RISK or INTERRUPTIONS FOR EMERGENCIES ONLY. Lastly, ask everyone except emergency staff to turn off their beepers.

#2 Double-Booking The Room

Double-booking can happen in many ways. You could forget to record a date on the master schedule or forget to tell the facility manager of your room needs. Or, someone else may preempt you and not let you know about it.

What's Wrong?

While you're out to lunch, the room could become an aerobics studio.

When you arrive for a 9 A.M. class you could find the room filled with visiting dignitaries.

Twenty people waiting in the hallway can cause a commotion.

You lose credibility with trainees.

Some Success Strategies:

Keep a copy of your room request document if a facility manager is involved. Confirm your room reservation three times: once two weeks in advance, then 48 hours in advance, and finally the day before the session is scheduled to begin. Jot down a note in your daily planner to remind yourself of dates to confirm.

#3 Wrong Rooms

Some training rooms aren't conducive to training. They're mainly used for other purposes such as for breaks, meals, board meetings or conferences.

What's Wrong?

These rooms are too small or too large and interfere with learning.

They don't have adequate soundproofing and privacy.

You can't arrange the environment to meet your needs.

Chances are you'll have trouble finding outlets for equipment.

There won't be a screen or adequate space for projections.

Some Success Strategies:

Do not assume anything about a training site. Ask to visit training locations in advance and be as flexible as you can, but stand your ground when the success of your program is compromised. Insist on site changes when necessary.

#4 The Usual Rooms

There is no reason to plan all your training programs in the typical classroom environment.

What's Wrong?

📄 A typical training room may not complement your training objectives.

📄 Learning is compromised when the site is wrong.

📄 Necessary equipment specific to the lessons may be missing.

📄 Your lack of planning demonstrates a lack of caring.

Some Success Strategies:

Think creatively when you plan programs, choosing places that are appropriate for the topic. For example, when people learn how to use software, they need to be in a room with computers rather than in a lecture hall looking at pictures of computers. And, training places don't always have to be rooms. Successful team building programs sometimes happen outdoors, in the woods, and on the rapids. Also in warehouses, bathrooms, buses and boardrooms.

#5 Locked Out

You just finished setting up your training room for the next day and you push the little button on the back of the door to lock up. Next morning you discover the keys you have only open the training room down the hall.

What's Wrong?

Time is wasted while you go look for someone to help.

You are perceived as absentminded or not careful.

Students get antsy and wonder if they should stay or leave.

Your strong and powerful opening is down the tube.

You feel stupid.

Some Success Strategies:

Never lock a door without first checking your keys. Be sure to keep a spare key in another place. Give the students a creative assignment while you seek help and consider sending someone out for food (*give them enough money for everyone*).

#6 Failing To Set "The Stage"

Failing to set *"the stage" (the area trainers use)* creates problems. An appropriate stage setting contributes to your success.

What's Wrong?

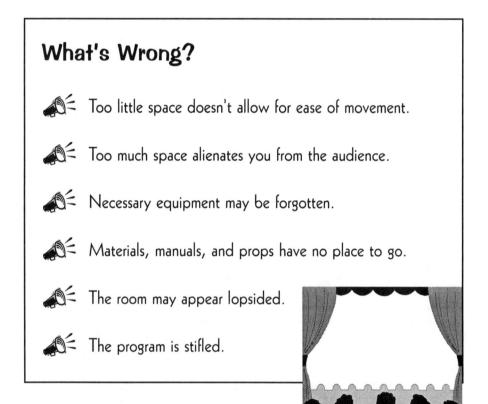

🔊 Too little space doesn't allow for ease of movement.

🔊 Too much space alienates you from the audience.

🔊 Necessary equipment may be forgotten.

🔊 Materials, manuals, and props have no place to go.

🔊 The room may appear lopsided.

🔊 The program is stifled.

Some Success Strategies:

Plan your *"acting space"* while you plan the program. If you're using an overhead projector, put it on a 6' table rather than a cart so you'll have room for overheads, manuals, props, etc. Leave 6' - 8' of space between you *(the table)* and the audience. Leave 4' - 6' between the table and the screen. If you're working off-site, give detailed instructions to the facility; provide a sketch, and arrive early to make adjustments. If you're on-site, arrive early and set the stage.

#7 Failing To Set "The House"

Failing to arrange *"the house" (the area in the room where participants sit)* can cause problems.

What's Wrong?

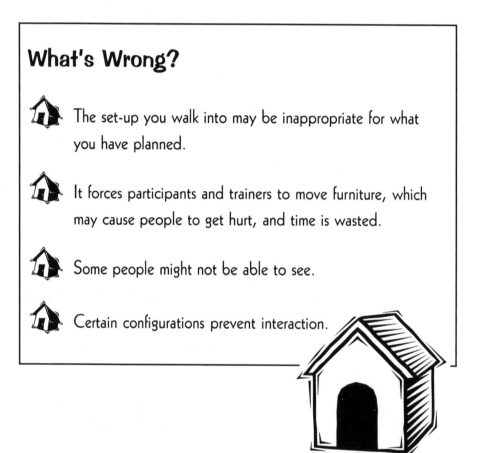

The set-up you walk into may be inappropriate for what you have planned.

It forces participants and trainers to move furniture, which may cause people to get hurt, and time is wasted.

Some people might not be able to see.

Certain configurations prevent interaction.

Some Success Strategies:

Plan the desired layout early and provide a *"house"* diagram to the facility manager. Be sure the layout matches learning objectives. Keep in mind that lecture/classroom style is the least effective for interaction. Horseshoe layout works best so people can see each other and can form break-out groups easily. Lastly, arrive early to make any necessary adjustments.

#8 Dark Rooms

Dark rooms are appropriate for developing film, for romantic encounters, and for movie theaters. Also for sleeping.

What's Wrong?

☆ Participants are invited to snooze in dark rooms.

☆ A safety hazard exists for everyone.

☆ It is difficult to take notes and read handouts with no light.

☆ Everyone loses eye contact with everyone else.

☆ Operating equipment in the dark is tricky.

☆ Light controls are hard to locate in the dark.

QUALITY
ASSUPANJE

Some Success Strategies:

Reconsider your need for a dark training room and eliminate the use of all equipment requiring dark rooms. Dim the lights if necessary, but not for long, and never immediately following a meal. Be sure a path is cleared for anyone entering the room, for emergency exits, or for trips to the restroom. When rooms have windows, keep the drapes or blinds open to allow natural lighting.

#9 Locked In

When you walk into the bathroom, a closet, or any other room and the door locks behind you, it means trouble.

What's Wrong?

🔒 Nobody knows where you are.

🔒 You'll lose valuable training time.

🔒 You look foolish and feel embarrassed.

🔒 You might have a panic attack.

🔒 If/when you get out, you will have a hard time picking up where you left off.

🔒 Everyone is distracted.

Some Success Strategies:

Check out your facility thoroughly before entering any rooms. Tell someone where you're going every time you go somewhere. As a precaution, take someone with you to wait outside. Consider carrying a cellular phone with you or keep a whistle in your pocket.

Chapter 2

How You Look And Act

#10 Dressing Inappropriately

Your clothing says a lot about you. People develop first impressions even before you say anything.

What's Wrong?

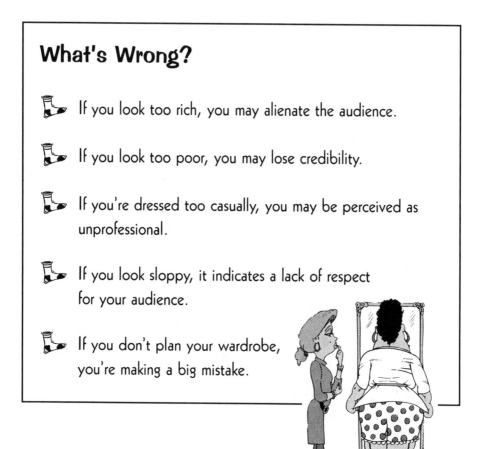

- If you look too rich, you may alienate the audience.

- If you look too poor, you may lose credibility.

- If you're dressed too casually, you may be perceived as unprofessional.

- If you look sloppy, it indicates a lack of respect for your audience.

- If you don't plan your wardrobe, you're making a big mistake.

Some Success Strategies:

Know your audience. Choose clothes that put you equal to or a notch above the audience. For example, if you're speaking to a group that will be suited up, suit up as well. If the group usually dresses in business casual attire, then dress about the same. For example, an Armani suit won't work for a group of front-line manufacturing employees.

#11 Not Flushing Out Hostages

Hostages are people mandated to attend the training program. They don't want to be there. They may be an entire class or only a few individuals. Ignore hostages and you'll be sorry!

What's Wrong?

☹ Hostages interfere with the learning process.

☹ Hostages shoot *"dagger eyes"* at the trainer causing discomfort.

☹ Hostages bully and intimidate those who want to learn.

☹ Hostages are no fun!

Some Success Strategies:

Acknowledge hostages in the beginning. After your powerful opening, when you're heading into discussing course objectives, take a light-hearted tone of voice and ask, *"How many of you are hostages, people who were told to be here?"* Follow with a discussion of the benefits of attending the training, and end with something like, *"Well, wherever you go, there you are, so you might as well be here!"* Make sure your tone of voice is cheerful!

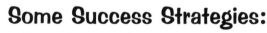

#12 Ignoring Grandstanders

Students will often go off on their soapboxes during a program. Trainers will often ignore this, letting it go on and on because they think it's a way to keep the audience involved.

What's Wrong?

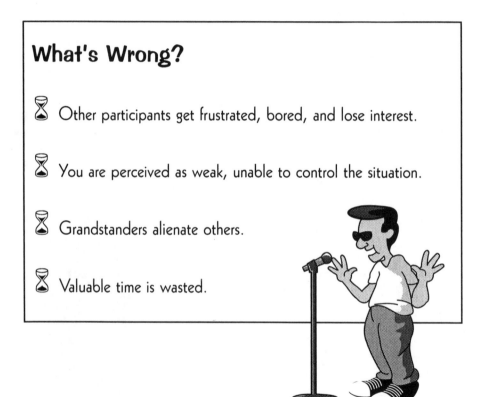

⏳ Other participants get frustrated, bored, and lose interest.

⏳ You are perceived as weak, unable to control the situation.

⏳ Grandstanders alienate others.

⏳ Valuable time is wasted.

Some Success Strategies:

At the first signal that grandstanding has begun, politely interrupt and ask how what is being said applies to the concepts being discussed. If the comments are relevant, allow the grandstander two to three minutes maximum to share his or her thoughts. When comments are clearly unrelated, politely ask that they be saved until the break. If grandstanding persists, move to the other side of the room. If this doesn't work, approach the person, explain the effect this behavior is having on the group and ask him to stop. And if none of this works, call 911!

#13 Being Someplace Else

The power is in the present moment. Being someplace else in your mind means you are not focused on the task at hand. When you're concerned about yesterday or tomorrow while you are training today, you are not in the present moment.

What's Wrong?

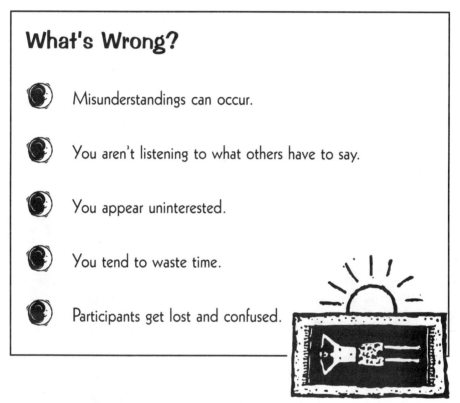

- Misunderstandings can occur.

- You aren't listening to what others have to say.

- You appear uninterested.

- You tend to waste time.

- Participants get lost and confused.

Some Success Strategies:

Pay attention to what you say to yourself. As soon as you find yourself drifting, silently say *"BE HERE NOW."* Practice sitting alone in a quiet place at least 15 minutes a day taking deep breaths and relaxing. You'll learn to experience PMA *(Present Moment Awareness)* so you can use it in the classroom when you're drifting to bring you back into what's happening now.

#14 Hiding Behind The Lectern

Trainers who stand behind the lectern, clutch the lectern, and lean on the lectern sabotage their success.

What's Wrong?

☞ Your body language is limited.

☞ Without body language, the clarity of your message is reduced.

☞ Short people disappear.

☞ There's a tendency to speak to the top of the lectern, rather than to the group.

☞ You place a barrier between yourself and the audience.

Some Success Strategies:

Step away from the lectern and move around the room or space. Your movement will keep learners more alert. If you must be near a lectern, then keep your notes on top of it and stand to the side.

#15 Being Impersonal

This means you avoid personal contact with your audience before and after your session. You also ignore them during breaks and interactive segments. Additionally, you make no effort to learn and use their names.

What's Wrong?

- Your credibility may suffer if you appear to be unapproachable.

- Being impersonal decreases their comfort level with you.

- You put up walls that deter learning.

- Trainees expect you to be available if they want to talk with you.

- Interaction is discouraged without name badges or name cards.

Some Success Strategies:

Talk with people at every opportunity. To show you notice and care, learn to say people's names properly. Ask trainees to wear name identification cards or use tent cards. Suggest printing names large enough for everyone to see. If you are shy, take a class or get a coach to help you improve your social skills. Tell trainees when you will be available for questions and discussion.

#16 Being Insensitive

People are different. Not everyone sees, hears, gets around, learns, and communicates in the same ways. Trainers can easily forget this.

What's Wrong?

- 😊 If you offend people, they stop learning from you.

- 😊 Disregarding individual *(learning needs)* blocks learning.

- 😊 Ignoring differences decreases your credibility.

- 😊 Neglecting to provide for different learning styles is the mark of an amateur.

- 😊 Overlooking differences in abilities is unprofessional.

Some Success Strategies:

Position yourself so you can communicate with everyone. Ask people who need special accommodations to inform you, and then ask them for specific ways to help them learn. During your session, keep asking for reminders if someone needs you to do something differently. Continuously ask for feedback: *"Can you all see me?" "Did everyone hear that?"*

#17 Being Clumsy

Holding a pointer while gesturing, falling into a freestanding screen, tripping over electrical cords and knocking props off the table are a few of the clumsy things trainers can do.

What's Wrong?

You appear incompetent and inept.

Participants begin to worry about you.

You could get hurt.

Participants could get hurt.

The facility can be damaged.

Equipment may get broken.

Some Success Strategies:

Pay attention at all times; watch what you are doing. Make sure your shoes fit and your shoelaces are tied. Put props in the middle of the table, and tape cables to the floor to avoid tripping. Put the pointer down after you have pointed. Stay away from caffeine; drink decaffeinated coffee and herbal tea, and pass on the chocolate doughnuts.

#18 Being In A Tizzy

A trainer in a tizzy is a trainer out of control.

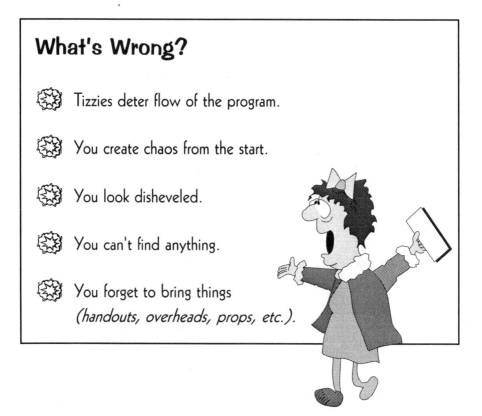

What's Wrong?

⚙ Tizzies deter flow of the program.

⚙ You create chaos from the start.

⚙ You look disheveled.

⚙ You can't find anything.

⚙ You forget to bring things
(handouts, overheads, props, etc.).

Some Success Strategies:

Don't procrastinate; plan all details of the program in advance. Create visual aids early in the preparation phase. Prepare a complete checklist of everything needed and review it at least 48 hours before the session. Ask a colleague to help by reminding you to bring needed things, and if possible, take everything to the training room a day early.

#19 Going Ballistic

Losing your temper, yelling at trainees, or becoming defensive is a sure way to sabotage your success.

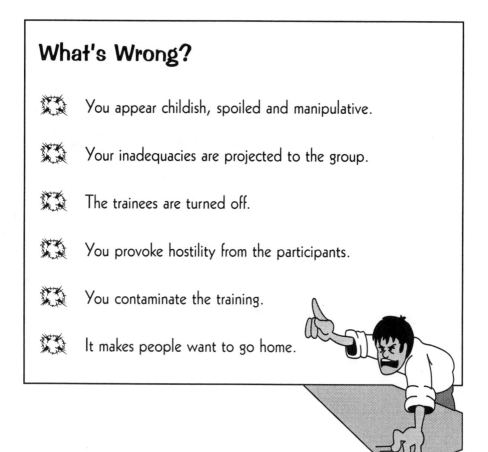

What's Wrong?

- You appear childish, spoiled and manipulative.
- Your inadequacies are projected to the group.
- The trainees are turned off.
- You provoke hostility from the participants.
- You contaminate the training.
- It makes people want to go home.

Some Success Strategies:

Pay attention to your body, breathe deeply, and stay calm. Step back and think before you speak. Practice PMA *(Present Moment Awareness);* stay focused. Acknowledge your feelings without losing self-control. Take a *"time-out."* Finally, apologize to the trainees if you lose self-control.

#20 No Eye Contact

Trainers look down, look to the side, look through or look over people and never make direct eye contact with the audience.

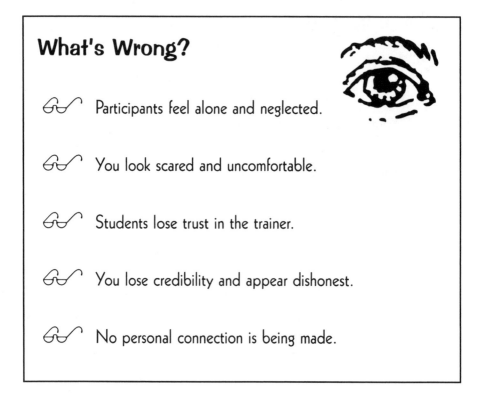

What's Wrong?

🖎 Participants feel alone and neglected.

🖎 You look scared and uncomfortable.

🖎 Students lose trust in the trainer.

🖎 You lose credibility and appear dishonest.

🖎 No personal connection is being made.

Some Success Strategies:

Commit to connecting with everyone. As you speak, look directly into someone's eyes for a few seconds and then move on to someone else. Be careful not to play tennis with your eyes (*gazing from right to left only*). When you're at the screen, talk to the audience, not to the screen. Remember what it feels like when someone won't look you in the eye while talking to you.

#21 Distracting Digits

Finger-pointing and finger-shaking while talking is offensive to listeners. Specific finger movements convey threatening or inappropriate messages. Using one or both hands to *"conduct"* the message is for symphony conductors only.

What's Wrong?

👉 Finger-pointing says scolding.

👉 *"I am superior"* is conveyed.

👉 These gestures contradict positive messages.

👉 Finger-pointing is distracting.

👉 *"Conducting"* blocks facial expressions.

Some Success Strategies:

Be aware of yourself and your gestures. Use video feedback to determine positive and negative gesturing. Eliminate finger-pointing, finger-waving, and hand-waving body language. Every time you notice you are waving or pointing, stop. Learn to break the habit.

#22 Faking Gestures

Have you ever seen bad acting? Have you ever noticed how beauty queens wave at crowds from parade floats? It's hard to describe faked gestures, but everyone knows them when they see them.

What's Wrong?

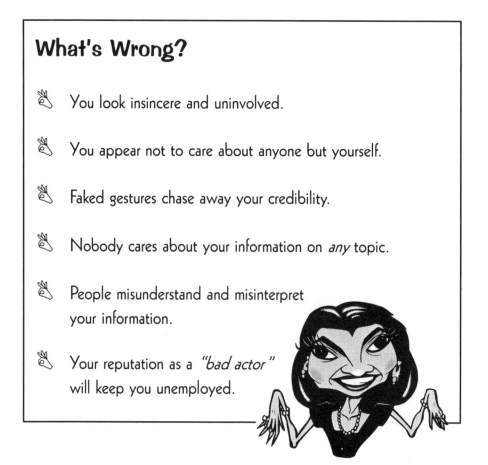

- You look insincere and uninvolved.

- You appear not to care about anyone but yourself.

- Faked gestures chase away your credibility.

- Nobody cares about your information on *any* topic.

- People misunderstand and misinterpret your information.

- Your reputation as a *"bad actor"* will keep you unemployed.

Some Success Strategies:

Don't worry about gesturing; just do it. Be yourself, move naturally, and learn to focus on your audience. Get comfortable with your subject-matter and with people. Be aware of your environment. Know what you're doing at all times. Find someone to coach you, take acting classes, or watch yourself on videotape.

#23 Getting In Their Faces

Trainers who stand too close to participants during a discussion get in their faces.

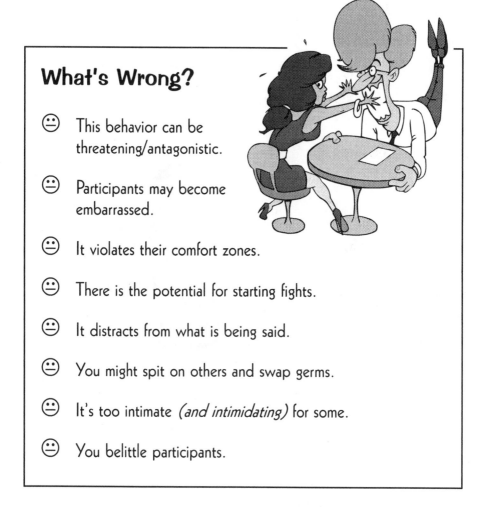

What's Wrong?

🙂 This behavior can be threatening/antagonistic.

🙂 Participants may become embarrassed.

🙂 It violates their comfort zones.

🙂 There is the potential for starting fights.

🙂 It distracts from what is being said.

🙂 You might spit on others and swap germs.

🙂 It's too intimate *(and intimidating)* for some.

🙂 You belittle participants.

Some Success Strategies:

Be sensitive to people's different personal bubbles. Some people don't mind if you get close to them, and others hate it. Stay on the outside edge of students' comfort zones. You'll know by observing their reactions to you. When they pull away or look away, back off!

#24 Spitting At Them

Trainers may get too excited and spit at audience members. People sitting in the front of the room or closest to the trainer get a shower instead of a lesson.

What's Wrong?

- It's disgusting.

- It's rude.

- It's unhealthy.

- It's unprofessional.

- It's a sure way to lose people.

- It's embarrassing for everyone.

Some Success Strategies:

Swallow often. If you have a problem with your teeth, see a dentist. Don't get so excited during your program you lose control. Pace yourself. Pay attention to the audience; if people are wiping their faces, step back a few feet. Remember to apologize to them. DON'T SPIT!

#25 The Chews

Candy, gum, tobacco, paper clips, toothpicks, and food in your mouth while you are speaking may seem like a good idea. IT'S NOT!

What's Wrong?

🍬 You can't hide what's in your mouth.

🍬 You appear unprofessional and uncaring.

🍬 People will wonder about your manners and your upbringing.

🍬 With your mouth full, they can't clearly hear what you're saying.

🍬 It's distracting behavior and they're likely to tune out.

French Fries

Some Success Strategies:

If you need to keep your throat lubricated, have a glass of water nearby. *(If you have a small bladder, don't drink too much, just take occasional sips)*. Suck on a piece of hard candy during the break if you want to, but be sure to finish it before you start again. Never chew tobacco, gum, toothpicks, paper clips or pencils. In the training environment, your mouth is meant for speaking, not for eating.

Chapter 3

Things You Say Or Hear

#26 "Today's Topic Is..."

Opening a training session with *"We're here today to talk about..."* is a poor beginning.

What's Wrong?

- This won't arouse or generate interest in the subject matter.

- It assumes participants don't know why they came to the class.

- The audience wonders if the trainer needs to be reminded of the program topic.

- It's just plain boring.

Some Success Strategies:

Ask engaging questions related to the topic (e.g., *"How many of you have ever ...?"*). Fire off some powerful statistics relevant to your subject. Refer to a recent event or incident that relates to the topic. Tell a story associated with the subject matter. Think creatively and remember you never have a second chance to make a first impression.

#27 I'm Perfect!

Trainers who present themselves as knowing everything and having all the answers are setting themselves up for failure.

What's Wrong?

☆ You demonstrate how insecure you really feel.

☆ You come across as a big phony.

☆ You look like you need to impress them.

☆ Any chance for establishing credibility is gone.

☆ Nobody's perfect!

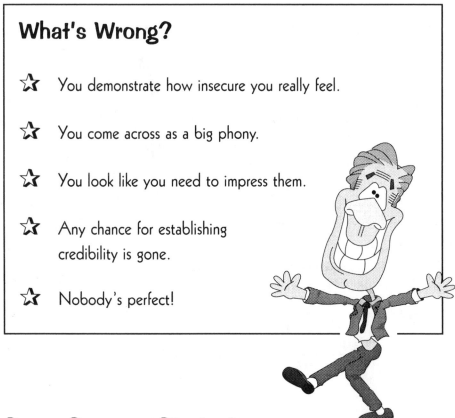

Some Success Strategies:

Remember, since nobody's perfect, you don't have to be. Don't agree to teach a class when you know you can't. Admit when you don't know something: *"That's a good question; I don't know the answer, but I'll find out and get back to you."* Tell them you have some answers, but not all the answers. Ask the audience to share what they know. You just might learn something too!

#28 Making Excuses

"The workbooks aren't collated because the copy machine went down." "We can't do the exercise because my dog ate the master copy." Excuses like these set you up for failure.

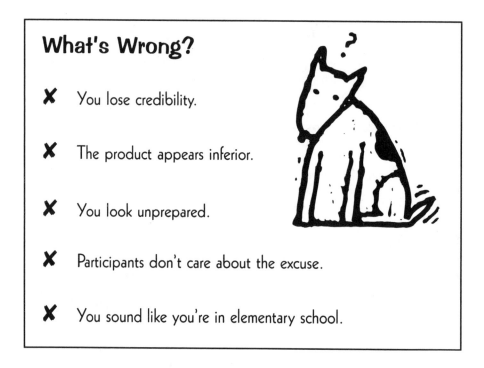

What's Wrong?

✗   You lose credibility.

✗   The product appears inferior.

✗   You look unprepared.

✗   Participants don't care about the excuse.

✗   You sound like you're in elementary school.

Some Success Strategies:

Don't wait until the last minute to prepare materials. Keep a back-up file of copies of exercises you often use on disk and on paper. Be sure to plan ahead for everything that can go wrong. Use a commercial copy service if necessary *(some are open 24 hours)*.

#29 Double Messages

When trainers say one thing and mean another, there's trouble. *"I run an informal program. It's kind of a casual day. However, I expect you to stay at your tables and hold your bladders until the break."*

What's Wrong?

"I run an informal program"

"stay at your tables and hold your bladders until the break."

👎 The audience is immediately confused and alienated.

👎 They wonder about your integrity.

👎 They feel like children who have to raise their hand to ask permission to go to the restroom.

👎 They talk and laugh about you behind your back.

👎 Your credibility is shot; you might as well go home.

Some Success Strategies:

Your ability to communicate effectively is critical to your success. Think before you speak and be consistent. Remember the golden rule and treat others as you want to be treated. *(Holding your bladder is not healthy and people need to move around once in a while).* So, just say what you mean and mean what you say.

#30 Using MEAPLES

A MEAPLE is any phrase, word, acronym, or abbreviation that has different meanings for different people. For example, PC means personal computer to some, while it means press conference or politically correct to others. A staple means one thing to a grocer and another to an office worker.

What's Wrong?

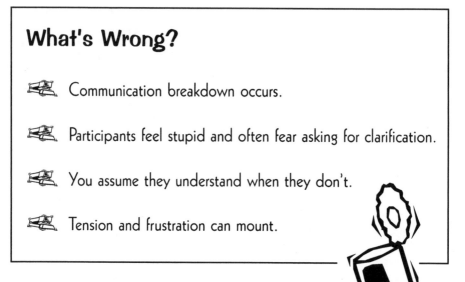

 Communication breakdown occurs.

Participants feel stupid and often fear asking for clarification.

You assume they understand when they don't.

Tension and frustration can mount.

Some Success Strategies:

As a trainer, never assume anything. Be on the lookout for MEAPLES; think before you speak. Use the complete word or phrase. Define the MEAPLE. If a MEAPLE slips out, read participants' non-verbal signals and clarify immediately. Remember, meanings are in people, not in words.

#31 Using Weak Words

"Try" and *"hopefully"* are weak words. For example, *"We'll try to achieve these five objectives today." "Hopefully, by the end of the session, you will have a departmental action plan."*

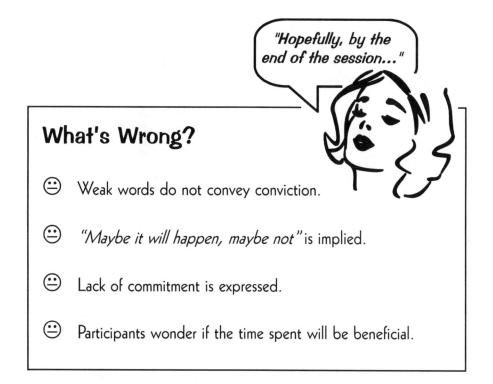

"Hopefully, by the end of the session..."

What's Wrong?

🙂 Weak words do not convey conviction.

🙂 *"Maybe it will happen, maybe not"* is implied.

🙂 Lack of commitment is expressed.

🙂 Participants wonder if the time spent will be beneficial.

Some Success Strategies:

Omit weak words from your vocabulary and replace them with *"do"* or *"will."* Remember what Ken Blanchard and Norman Vincent Peale said, *"Trying is just a noisy way of not doing."* Instead, say *"We will achieve these five objectives today,"* and *"By the end of the session, you will have a departmental action plan."*

#32 Using Fuzzy Words & Phrases

Fuzzy words are imprecise. They mean something different to every person and lead to confusion and conflict. How often is *"frequently"* or *"usually?"* When is *"soon"* or *"sometime?"* When was *"recently"* or *"a while ago?"*

What's Wrong?

"Sometime soon"

- ✍ You assume trainees know what you mean.

- ✍ You act as if they are mind readers *(they're not)*.

- ✍ You create conflict.

- ✍ They misunderstand.

- ✍ They get to blame you for giving them bad information.

- ✍ You get defensive when they do.

Some Success Strategies:

Clarify fuzzy words and phrases. If you hear a fuzzy word or phrase, ask *"Do you mean...?"* Agree on an exact date or time or amount, and repeat it to each other. Use precise words instead.

#33 Using Minimizers & Qualifiers

"Think," "might," "perhaps" and *"maybe"* are minimizers and qualifiers. They minimize and qualify what you say. *"I think we might have a productive session."* *"Perhaps we'll end at 4 P.M. so maybe we can beat the traffic."*

What's Wrong?

☐ These words promote communication breakdown.

☐ They are too vague.

☐ They diminish the value of the response.

☐ They don't project confidence or commitment.

☐ The listener is left wondering what was meant.

SEMINAR

Some Success Strategies:

Like weak words, omit these words from your vocabulary. Take a stand; make a commitment. Be specific so that the listener is clear about what you mean. *"Today's session will be productive."* *We'll end at four so you can beat the traffic."*

#34 Monotones & Mumbles

Trainers will sabotage their success when they speak in monotones and don't articulate clearly.

What's Wrong?

♦ You appear insecure, with limited self-esteem.

♦ Communication breakdown occurs.

♦ Participants struggle to understand.

♦ The audience loses interest quickly and tunes out.

♦ The delivery is boring.

Some Success Strategies:

To overcome mumbles and monotones, practice delivering your presentation into a tape recorder or on video. Listen carefully and ask yourself if you would want to listen to you. Repeat tongue twisters quickly while concentrating on clear articulation. For example, *"She sells sea shells by the sea shore." "A proper cup of coffee in a copper coffee pot."* Repeat the above tongue twisters emphasizing different words each time. To add pizzazz to your voice, vary the speed and volume. Pause or speak softer when you want to make an important point. Be sure there's variety in your voice.

#35 Speech Tics

Trainers use speech tics when they repeatedly use their favorite phrases such as *"okay," "ya know," "I'll tell ya what,"* and *"I mean,"* etc.

What's Wrong?

♦   *"Speech tics"* are annoying to the audience.

♦   Repetitive sounds get old and boring fast.

♦   Trainees get easily distracted.

♦   They will start counting your *"speech tics."*

♦   Some people will make fun of you.

♦   You decrease your believability.

Some Success Strategies:

Recognize your pet phrases and work on eliminating them. Ask someone to keep a record each and every time one slips out. Videotape or audiotape yourself. Listen for your *"speech tics"* so you are more aware of when and how you use them. Hire a speech coach or take a speech improvement class so you can break the habit.

#36 They Can't Hear You

Some trainers think if they scream at the audience, they will command attention and project power. Others think if they whisper, the audience will work harder to pay attention and therefore, more learning will take place. Neither is right.

What's Wrong?

🔊 Audiences withdraw when they can't hear the trainer.

🔊 Listening to a trainer speaking too loudly conjures up uncomfortable childhood memories of being yelled at; it's demeaning.

🔊 When you speak too loudly you may spit on trainees.

🔊 Speaking too loudly or too softly is irritating and interferes with learning.

Some Success Strategies:

Since 40 percent of your ability to successfully transfer your message to the listener relates to the volume, rate and pitch of your voice, you need to find a mid-range that is comfortable for both you and your audience. Tape record yourself, videotape yourself, and ask others for feedback because how you say what you say matters.

#37 "Trust Me"

Saying *"Take my word for it,"* *"Just do what I say,"* or *"I guarantee the results"* is like saying *"Eat this, it'll be good for you."*

What's Wrong?

- These phrases imply trainees don't have minds of their own.

- You project a certain element of superiority.

- It sounds like you're too lazy to explain things in detail.

- Your job is to teach, not to preach.

Some Success Strategies:

Establish your credibility early and be done with it. Invite trainees to experiment with your recommendations. Show them why the concept is important, and then show them how to implement the idea. Involve them in their own learning. Finally, ask them to determine the potential benefits.

#38 "Learn This Or Else"

In training adults, using fear, threatening, and pulling rank don't work. For example, saying, *"If you don't learn this material, you won't get promoted."*

What's Wrong?

☆ Trainees tend to turn into rebellious children.

☆ They say, *"I may hear it, but you can't make me learn it."*

☆ Lessons go in short-term memory, not in long-term memory.

☆ People aren't motivated by fear.

☆ Pulling rank turns people off.

Some Success Strategies:

If training must be mandatory, present it in a positive way. Provide options so trainees feel they have some control over their situation. Be sure to show trainees how the program will benefit them. Get all participants involved in the beginning of the program. Show them how to apply the content. Most importantly, don't ever make threats.

#39 "Oh, I Forgot To Tell You..."

While your trainees move around talking and forming small task groups according to your instructions, you suddenly remember something important you forgot to tell them.

What's Wrong?

? You are interrupting and disturbing them.

? You appear inept and unprepared.

? You will have trouble getting their attention back to you.

? The room is so noisy they don't hear you and the exercise becomes confusing.

? You waste time.

? They get frustrated.

"I Forgot"

Some Success Strategies:

After your instructions, but before participants begin the activity, say, *"Let me make sure I told you everything you need to know before you begin this activity."* Have detailed instructions printed on a handout to give to each group. Post instructions on the flip chart or the overhead projector. Don't interrupt them once they've begun.

#40 "Did Ya Hear The One About...?"

It's a mistake to preface your jokes and stories with lead-ins like, *"Did ya hear the one about...?"*

What's Wrong?

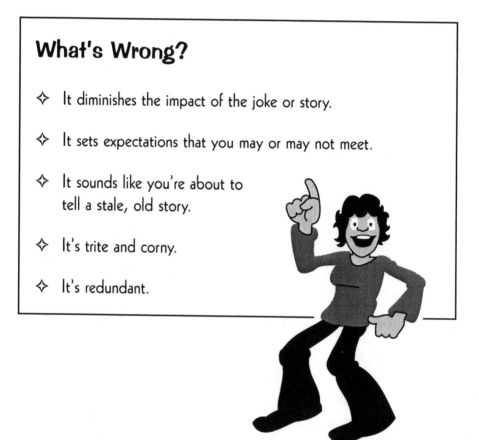

✧ It diminishes the impact of the joke or story.

✧ It sets expectations that you may or may not meet.

✧ It sounds like you're about to tell a stale, old story.

✧ It's trite and corny.

✧ It's redundant.

Some Success Strategies:

The worst ways to get into a joke or story are *"Oh, did ya hear the one about...?"* and *"Did I already tell you about...?"* and *"You're going to love this one...."* Good joke tellers and storytellers don't announce their jokes and stories. Instead, they just tell the joke or story with no lead-in.

---

41 Using Inappropriate Humor

Humor that offends your audience is far worse than no humor at all. Trouble is, we often don't know when we've used offensive humor. Worse, sometimes we don't care (e.g., "That's your problem buster," "I didn't mean it that way," or "Can't you take a joke?").

What's Wrong?

People stop learning from us after we offend them.

Being insensitive to others is unprofessional.

Your credibility takes a nose-dive.

It could land you in court.

Some Success Strategies:

Ask several people for their advice about using your funny material. In particular, ask people who are different from you, and whose sense of humor is different from yours. Take their advice seriously. And don't forget to analyze your audience very carefully. If you have any doubt about something you think is appropriate, don't say it. Edit your mouth!

#42 Being Funny When You're Not

Sometimes trainers decide to tell a joke, drag out a rubber chicken, or show a cartoon just to lighten up a program.

What's Wrong?

- You forget you're a trainer, not a comedian.

- You don't bother to get good material.

- You expect divine inspiration.

- You think good laugh lines come naturally.

- When you bomb, you blame the audience. *(They didn't get it.)*

- You forget that impromptu humor takes lots of practice.

Some Success Strategies:

Tie humor to your training objectives. Prepare funny material in advance. Remember to use humorous material you really like. Practice telling your jokes and stories until you tell them with exactly the effect you want. Ask an expert to help you get it right.

#43 Lousy Story Topics

Your stories and anecdotes all have the same theme, maybe sports, cooking, automobiles, gardening, or children.

What's Wrong?

◆ You incorrectly assume everyone shares your interests.

◆ You are alienating a portion of your audience.

◆ People may not understand the jargon you use.

◆ You may appear gender-biased and lose credibility.

◆ The audience is drained or bored listening to the same theme over and over.

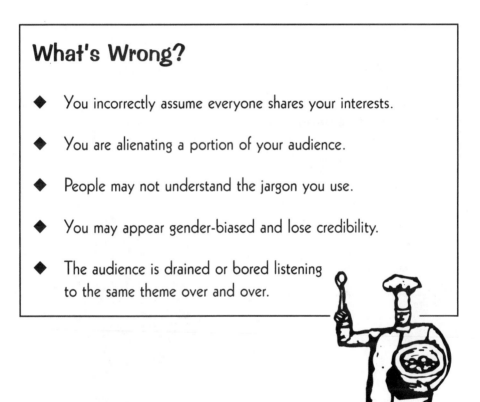

Some Success Strategies:

Survey the audience before the training begins or during an icebreaker activity. Find out what their hobbies and interests are. Vary the topics of your stories and anecdotes in an effort to include everyone. For a change of pace, ask participants to share stories about their experiences.

#44 No "Hip-Pocket" Stories

It's an oversight to think nothing unexpected will happen. And, it's worse not to be prepared for it with something to lighten the mood.

What's Wrong?

☆ You stumble, fumble, and mumble.

☆ You look unprofessional.

☆ You lose control of the program.

☆ Participants become concerned about your ability to fix what's wrong.

Some Success Strategies:

Anticipate what is most likely to go wrong and prepare stories, anecdotes or jokes to help with those situations. Make sure your stories break the tension and move your program forward. You can even take a folded-up paper from your hip pocket and refer to it for reminders of your *"impromptu"* remarks.

#45 "The Research Indicates..."

While conducting a discussion, trainers may say, *"The research indicates..."* or *"Psychologists say..."* What research and which psychologists?

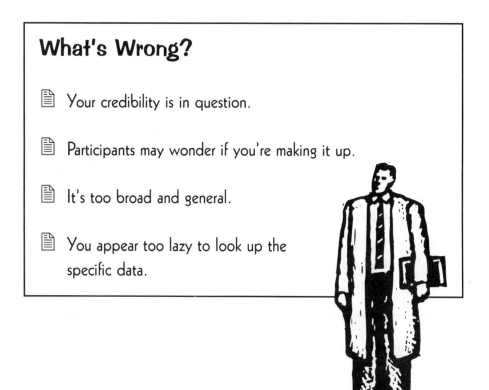

What's Wrong?

📄 Your credibility is in question.

📄 Participants may wonder if you're making it up.

📄 It's too broad and general.

📄 You appear too lazy to look up the specific data.

Some Success Strategies:

If you want to quote research, be sure to specify when the study took place, where it was conducted, who collected the data and how the results were achieved. Regarding psychologists or other professionals you want to discuss, indicate their names and backgrounds. If you can't remember where the data came from, don't use it.

#46 No Bridges

Jumping from topic to topic and forgetting to summarize with clear transitions means participants have to jump with you without the benefit of a bridge.

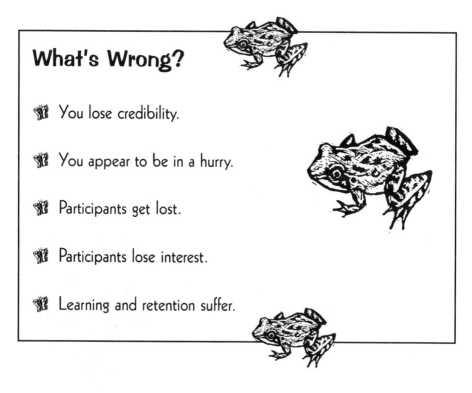

What's Wrong?

- 🦋 You lose credibility.

- 🦋 You appear to be in a hurry.

- 🦋 Participants get lost.

- 🦋 Participants lose interest.

- 🦋 Learning and retention suffer.

Some Success Strategies:

Build bridges into your program notes. Ask students to summarize key points of the section. Create a breakout activity that summarizes the section. Give a five-point summary quiz orally to the whole class. Simply state the summary and tie it in to the next section.

#47 Entering The Tangent Zone

Trainers often digress, change the subject and get lost in the tangent zone, unable to find their way back home.

What's Wrong?

♦ Participants get lost, too!

♦ You appear unorganized.

♦ Confusion reigns and lessons are skewed.

♦ The audience wonders if you have enough material to fill the time.

♦ Participants lose interest.

Some Success Strategies:

Although it's okay to digress a bit, be sure to return quickly. One tangent can lead to another tangent and can lead to another tangent. If you are consciously aware of each moment, you'll be able to know that it's time to leave the tangent zone and return to the program. Do so by summarizing the digression and pick up where you left off.

#48 This is MY Life

When trainers tell too many personal stories, the audience can feel like they tuned into a TV show entitled *This is MY Life.*

What's Wrong?

- You run the risk of entering *The Tangent Zone.*

- Participants perceive your ego to be bigger than Mt. Everest.

- Program focus gets lost.

- It feels like you're wasting time.

- Or, maybe you just like to hear yourself talk.

Some Success Strategies:

Only tell personal stories that are truly relevant to the topic. Keep them short and to the point. Tell no more than two per full-day program. Practice your stories before dumping them on an audience. Ask colleagues for feedback *(e.g., does the story work?)*. If it's a heavy story, find a way to return to levity.

#49 Ignoring The Others

The trainer gets caught up in dialogue with only one trainee.

What's Wrong?

☹ The rest of the group is alienated.

☹ They nod out, tune out, or trickle out.

☹ Ignoring others can lead to their anger or hostility.

☹ You lose control of the session.

☹ Valuable time is wasted.

Some Success Strategies:

Recognize when you are having a private discussion in public. Explain that this type of a discussion isn't appropriate now. Tell the trainee you'll be glad to continue the discussion during the next break. Politely invite input from others in the group. Ask open-ended questions to encourage discussion from others. Change the subject and move on.

#50 Shunning Questions

It's a stupid thing to ignore audience questions or to discourage people from asking them.

What's Wrong?

♦ Dialogue is needed to ensure learning.

♦ People don't always understand what you think you said.

♦ Telling them what you think they need to know isn't enough.

♦ Ignoring audience input means missing important information.

Some Success Strategies:

Be sure to invite and model interaction. Ask for questions as you go through your material. Respond to all questions with respect and useful information, but avoid thanking questioners (*i.e., "Thank you for asking that."*). And avoid giving ratings such as, *"That's the best question so far today."*

#51 Cutting Off Questions

Asking for additional information or clarification is part of the learning process. To stand in the way of the learning process is exactly the opposite of why trainers go to work.

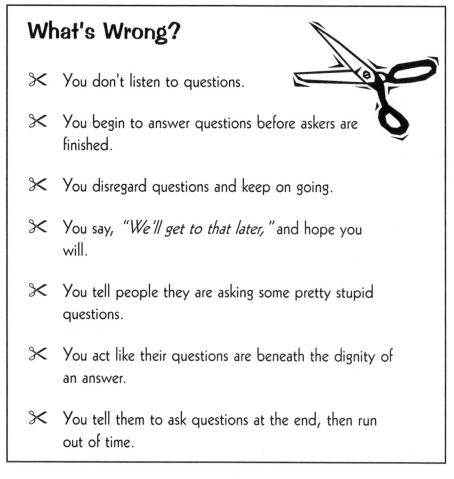

What's Wrong?

✂ You don't listen to questions.

✂ You begin to answer questions before askers are finished.

✂ You disregard questions and keep on going.

✂ You say, *"We'll get to that later,"* and hope you will.

✂ You tell people they are asking some pretty stupid questions.

✂ You act like their questions are beneath the dignity of an answer.

✂ You tell them to ask questions at the end, then run out of time.

Some Success Strategies:

State your preference for question-handling at the beginning. Honor questions as though they are gifts to you. Paraphrase questions so trainees know you understood. Listen to the entire question before responding. Be careful not to roll your eyes if you think it's a stupid question.

#52 Asking Only Closed Questions

Closed questions begin with *can, will, does/do, is/are, has/have*, etc. Using these, trainers maintain complete control of the conversation.

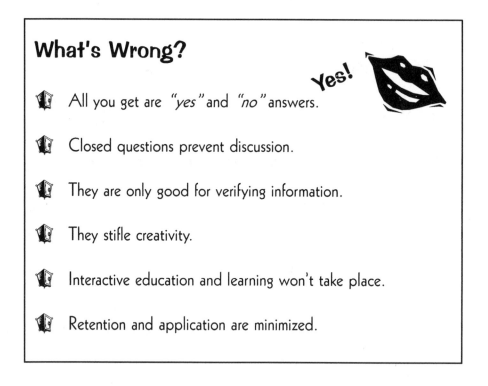

What's Wrong?

Yes!

- All you get are *"yes"* and *"no"* answers.

- Closed questions prevent discussion.

- They are only good for verifying information.

- They stifle creativity.

- Interactive education and learning won't take place.

- Retention and application are minimized.

 No!

Some Success Strategies:

If your intent is to take control of the conversation, use closed questions. However, to open the flow of information, use open-ended questions beginning with *what, how* and *why*. To stimulate further discussion, use statements beginning with *"Please explain,"* *"Tell me,"* and *"Elaborate on that."* And remember, adults learn while being involved.

#53 Affirming The Negative

Trainers who say, *"I don't want to be here anymore than you do,"* *"This is for your own good,"* or *"This is just another useless training program,"* affirm the negative.

What's Wrong?

Implanting negative thoughts produces negative results.

If you expect the worst you will get the worst.

Participants tune out.

Time is wasted.

Some Success Strategies:

If you're assigned a program you don't want to present, find another trainer to take your place. Or, try changing your attitude. You might look for something positive. Or, talk yourself into a successful experience. Take care to visualize positive results. Finally, express enthusiasm.

54 Negative Talk

"Don't forget to..." and *"Why don't we..."* are negative language phrases.

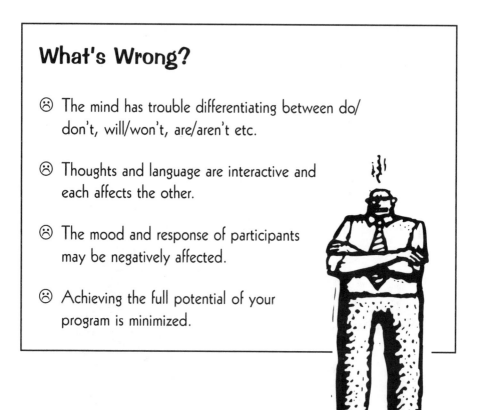

What's Wrong?

☹ The mind has trouble differentiating between do/ don't, will/won't, are/aren't etc.

☹ Thoughts and language are interactive and each affects the other.

☹ The mood and response of participants may be negatively affected.

☹ Achieving the full potential of your program is minimized.

Some Success Strategies:

Learn to use language as a tool to help maximize learning. Pay careful attention to your use of negative language. To break the habit and also teach the concept, ask participants to listen carefully for negative language. They can signal you when they hear it. Focus on the positive *(e.g., "Remember to..."* and *"Let's do ...").*

#55 Belittling Others

Trainers who make fun of trainees or the boss or the company belittle others. They make participants feel stupid for asking questions and daring to guess at answers. They put down people with different accents. They get into people-bashing, hobby-bashing, policies-bashing, etc.

What's Wrong?

- You automatically lose credibility.

- Participants will tune out forever.

- Belittling behavior is rude and insulting.

- It's offensive.

- It's cruel.

- It's never appropriate.

Some Success Strategies:

Remember your opinions are yours and it is not your job to share them. Recognize that not everyone shares your beliefs and opinions. When your motive is to feel *"more than"* the next person or group, you are saying something designed to make you feel better and someone else worse. Don't belittle anyone!

#56 No Respect

Trainers lecture to participants the entire time, say they don't have time for questions, make a big deal of their superior status, and tell others how to live their lives.

What's Wrong?

🎂 Telling others what to do without getting their input doesn't work.

🎂 No respect is shown for participants.

🎂 They become alienated and tune out.

🎂 You ignore and belittle their life experiences.

"Let Them Eat Cake!"

Some Success Strategies:

Ask others for their interests and opinions. Listen to what people have to say and don't interrupt. Avoid giving advice or telling others what to do. Ask open-ended questions to help people think about what you want them to learn, such as, *"What would it be like to implement this concept?"* rather than *"Do this and your life will be wonderful."*

#57 Gender Benders

It's a mistake for trainers to consistently refer to secretaries and nurses as females and to plumbers and managers as males. Women are never salesmen, policemen or mailmen.

What's Wrong?

- You're guilty of stereotyping and perpetuating old prejudices.

- You appear insensitive and offend participants.

- You fail to recognize that both men and women do all jobs.

- You're behind the times.

- You're sloppy about details.

Some Success Strategies:

Vary your use of he and she for all workers and refer to the work being done rather than who is doing it. *Say "salesperson," "police officer,"* or *"mail carrier."* Omit gender references. Instead of saying, *"He's a male nurse and she's a female plumber,"* say, *"He's a nurse and she's a plumber."* When in doubt, ask people what they prefer to be called.

#58 Using Brand Names

When you say, *"Xerox this page for everyone,"* and *"Be sure to have extra Kleenex,"* and *"Get a Coke for each person,"* it sounds like free advertising for those products.

What's Wrong?

- It is improper use of registered trademarks.

- A trademark is an adjective, not a verb or a noun.

- You appear careless with the property of others.

- You are sloppy about details and lose credibility.

- You can get sued for misuse.

Some Success Strategies:

Use generic names instead of brand names: for example, use *"photocopy"* for *"Xerox,"* *"tissue"* for *"Kleenex,"* and *"soft drink"* for *"Coke."* Avoid using specific product names to represent entire categories of products. Use trademarked brand names properly: for example, Ivory soap, Visa credit card, and Energizer brand batteries.

#59 Apologizing For Everything

"I'm sorry" sounds okay as a song title, but not so okay in a trainer's litany. *"I'm sorry the room is too cold/too hot." "I'm sorry the handouts/slides/props are so difficult to see." "I'm sorry, but it's time to start/stop now."*

"I'm sorry"

What's Wrong?

◆ You present an inferior product.

◆ You come across as a wimp.

◆ You sound like a broken record.

◆ Participants wonder if you'll get anything right.

◆ They don't care that you're sorry; they want things to work.

Some Success Strategies:

Plan ahead and prevent problems from occurring. If something isn't right, your job is to fix it. Ignore it rather than draw attention to it, especially if it isn't a big deal. Most importantly, stop apologizing for everything!

#60 "Porky Pig" Endings

Porky Pig used to say, *"That's all folks."* Trainers sometimes say, *"That's it for today, folks"* and *"Our time's up, folks"*. These are weak endings.

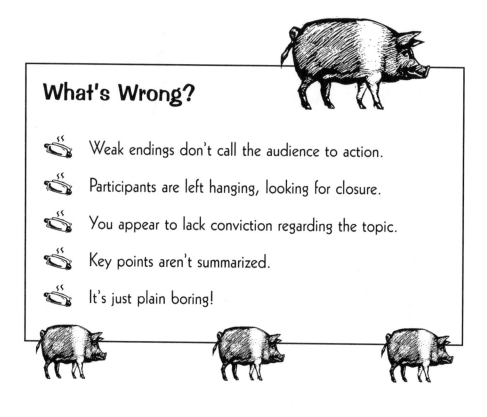

What's Wrong?

- Weak endings don't call the audience to action.

- Participants are left hanging, looking for closure.

- You appear to lack conviction regarding the topic.

- Key points aren't summarized.

- It's just plain boring!

Some Success Strategies:

Ask participants to share how they will apply new concepts. Make your main point one last time (*e.g., "Stupid things we do can sabotage our success."*). Then, pause a moment and move to the side. Close with a powerful relevant quotation or story. DON'T say, *"In conclusion..."*.

Chapter 4

Methods And Materials You Use

#61 No Background Information

The trainer neglects to learn about the needs of the group and what they already know about the topic.

What's Wrong?

📄 Training content is inappropriate and poorly received by the group.

📄 You miss an opportunity to connect with participants.

📄 Materials are too basic or too advanced.

📄 Communication breakdown occurs.

📄 You lose credibility.

Background

Some Success Strategies:

Conduct a survey in advance to determine the needs of the audience. Interview several people who will be attending. Research previous training conducted on similar topics. If you're an outside consultant, research the organization *(annual reports, etc.)*. Have lunch with some attendees before the training session. Ask for a list of organization *"buzzwords" (see #30 MEAPLES).*

#62 Being Lazy

Being lazy means creating a program once and using it over and over and over without changing anything. It also means buying a generic program from a training company and not doing anything to customize it for your audience.

What's Wrong?

- Unlike fine wine, training programs don't improve with age.

- Material becomes obsolete and outdated.

- You sound like you're bored with it.

- The workbook has turned yellow.

- The overheads are all scratched.

- Participants feel slighted.

Some Success Strategies:

Each time you use it, create at least one new case study, activity, transparency, flip chart page, handout, etc. After five years throw it out and start over. Apply CPI *(Continuous Process Improvement)* at all times. Finally, ask colleagues for new ideas.

#63 Winging It

You were scheduled to conduct the training several months ago and you kept saying, *"I've got lots of time to pull it together."* Time runs out and you have to wing it, and go in totally unprepared.

What's Wrong?

Don't kid yourself; the audience will know.

You look dazed and confused.

Little learning takes place.

You neglect to have any visual aids or handouts.

You look like a bad comedian doing improvisation.

You feel *"icky"* all day.

Some Success Strategies:

Start a file on the program as soon as you are scheduled to do it. Use a standard pre-program questionnaire that includes questions about the audience profile, course objectives, desired outcomes, logistics, necessary room set-up and audiovisual needs. Fill in the questionnaire during the initial conversation about the program. Plan at least two weeks to create handouts and visual aids.

#64 Foolish Icebreakers

When you took *Train the Trainer* somebody told you everyone likes to hop around on one foot and say hello to other people who are guessing what kind of insect they represent.

What's Wrong?

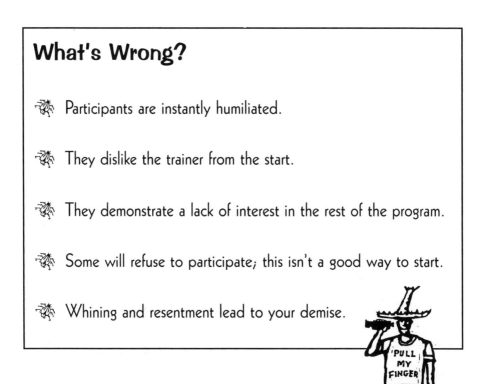

🐛 Participants are instantly humiliated.

🐛 They dislike the trainer from the start.

🐛 They demonstrate a lack of interest in the rest of the program.

🐛 Some will refuse to participate; this isn't a good way to start.

🐛 Whining and resentment lead to your demise.

Some Success Strategies:

Ask trainees to talk about why they are attending the class, and what they want to gain by the end of the day, etc. This can be done in a zip-around-the-room format, or in larger audiences, people can talk to three or four others. Read a book about icebreakers; rate them on the humiliation scale and select those that are the least threatening and humiliating. Ask other trainers for successful, non-foolish, icebreaker ideas. Never force anyone to do anything.

#65 Clutching The Workbook

The workbook or training manual is not a security blanket. It is a reference tool and should be used accordingly.

What's Wrong?

📖 You project a lack of confidence.

📖 Participants think you don't know the topic very well.

📖 It stifles a high energy delivery.

📖 You can't use your hands to gesture.

📖 It impedes positive posture.

📖 It's a barrier between you and the audience.

Some Success Strategies:

Study the material and know it cold. Request a table in the front of the room; leave the manual there and only refer back to it from time to time. Keep your hands free for gesturing. Have a one-page outline nearby to glance at. Put the outline on a flip chart page; hang it where it's visible.

#66 Reading

It's wrong to believe that nothing is wrong with reading your entire presentation. Go ahead, read your transparencies, too. Poetry, letters, and all handouts are other possibilities. Reading guarantees you will remember all the special words and thoughts you planned.

What's Wrong?

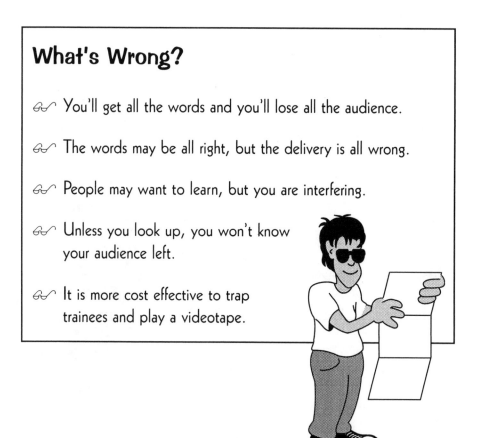

- ⤳ You'll get all the words and you'll lose all the audience.

- ⤳ The words may be all right, but the delivery is all wrong.

- ⤳ People may want to learn, but you are interfering.

- ⤳ Unless you look up, you won't know your audience left.

- ⤳ It is more cost effective to trap trainees and play a videotape.

Some Success Strategies:

Avoid reading aloud to audiences. Find ways to eliminate verbatim reading of more than two sentences. A few notable exceptions include when an entire group is together looking at a few words on paper or projected on a screen, and you must read these few words rather than paraphrasing them. Also, if you've got a short quote from someone famous, it's okay to read it.

#67 YAK YAK YAK

All the trainer does is lecture and talk at the audience, hour after hour after hour...

What's Wrong?

🔊 It's boring and is guaranteed to put people to sleep.

🔊 All the senses are not involved.

🔊 This is not interactive.

🔊 The learning process is impeded.

🔊 It's unimaginative.

Some Success Strategies:

Plan carefully. Include a variety of methods. Ask open-ended questions to generate discussion. Have breakout activities for small groups. Do self-assessment activities followed by discussion. Use colorful overheads, flip charts, and handouts. Show short videos appropriate to the subject matter. Have volunteers role-play short vignettes related to the topic.

#68 No Humor In It

Trainers are in trouble when they think their topic is too serious for adding humor, or that it's impossible to add humor to their program.

What's Wrong?

☹ You assume humor is only about telling jokes.

☹ You discount the importance of humor in learning retention.

☹ You overlook use of humor as a valuable teaching method.

☹ You present a boring, monotonous program.

Some Success Strategies:

Lighten up. Exercise your own sense of humor daily so you'll be ready if you need to be. Study how presenters you admire use humor and learn from them. Look for material that is funny to you and relevant to your topic and risk sharing it with others. Experiment with ways to integrate humor into your training. For example, tell an amusing story you read in a magazine and relate it to something you want them to learn.

#69 Forcing Role Play

A little bit of theater isn't a bad idea, however, when you cast reluctant performers, you're bound to get bad reviews.

What's Wrong?

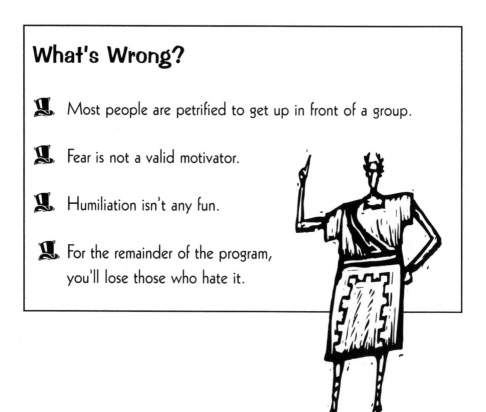

🎩 Most people are petrified to get up in front of a group.

🎩 Fear is not a valid motivator.

🎩 Humiliation isn't any fun.

🎩 For the remainder of the program, you'll lose those who hate it.

Some Success Strategies:

Ask for volunteers. If nobody volunteers, bribe them or skip it. Create small groups where the task is to demonstrate a concept learned in class. Everyone in the group has to participate, however, one can be the director, one the introducer, etc. Those who want to *"act"* will. Do a *"reader's theater"* exercise instead: groups write scripts and read to the class *(there's comfort in numbers)*.

#70 Too Much To Cover

When training is necessary because there's a lot of new information for people to know, you design a training program to cover everything in one day.

What's Wrong?

It's too complicated to understand all at once.

There's too much for trainees to learn.

There's no time to practice new behaviors.

Trainees don't get enough time to *"own"* the new material.

They only remember fragments of the information.

Some Success Strategies:

There are only three things for trainers to do when there's too much material to cover: simplify, simplify and simplify. An average person can only remember clusters of three or four concepts at a time. Break the material down into several shorter sessions spaced apart by at least a week so that trainees can digest and apply new concepts.

#71 Too Many Toys & Thrills

Learning is supposedly enhanced with the use of gimmicks, gadgets, games, gizmos, music, movement, magic, etc. Sometimes it is and sometimes it isn't.

What's Wrong?

◎   Too much of anything is overwhelming and can be distracting.

◎   Sensory overload can cause trainees to tune out.

◎   The entertainment becomes the focus and the lesson can get lost.

◎   Learning can be diminished.

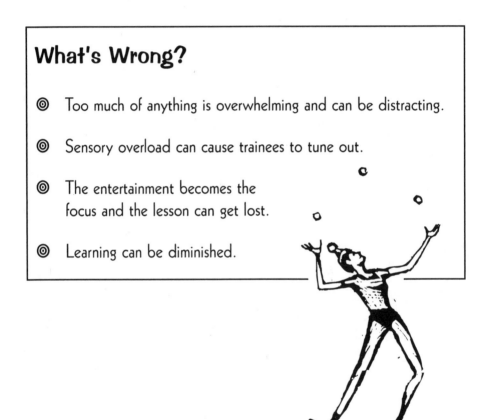

Some Success Strategies:

Tie all toys and thrills to specific learning objectives. Their purpose is to get learning to stick. For example, a magic trick can demonstrate the disappearance of coins and can also demonstrate the disappearance of company profits. Musical selections must match the mood you wish to create. For example, ocean sounds work better in Stress Management classes than loud rock and roll. If you choose to use toys and thrills, be sure they are generic enough to be recognized by everyone. And, don't use them just to use them. Less is more.

#72 Too Many Breakouts

Every hour on the hour the trainer says, *"Break into small groups and do this exercise for 30 minutes. We'll debrief it for 15 minutes and then take a 15-minute break."*

What's Wrong?

✔ Participants wonder why you're even there.

✔ You look like you don't know how to teach.

✔ Audience involvement is one thing; excess is another.

✔ CBT *(Computer-Based Training)* programs would be more cost-effective.

✔ You're lazy.

Some Success Strategies:

Balance the number of breakouts with other teaching methods. Be sure all breakouts are tied to specific learning objectives. Plan breakouts that are fun as well as enlightening. Know your audience and gauge their expertise or interest in such activities. If they hate them, don't use them. Make sure the size of the group is appropriate for the activity.

#73 Sensory Deprivation

The trainer lectures in a monotone without any visual aids, body movement or interaction with the audience.

What's Wrong?

☠ Participants fall asleep within a few minutes.

☠ Learning is not personalized.

☠ Trainees don't participate so they don't learn.

☠ Lack of variety is boring.

☠ You look bored with the topic and the audience.

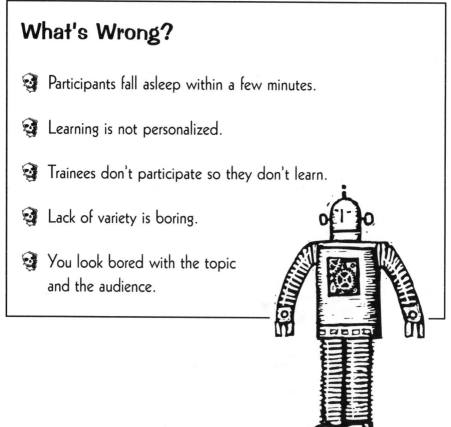

Some Success Strategies:

Recognize that people learn in different ways: some prefer to see information, some prefer to hear information, and some prefer to experience information. It is important to provide something for everyone. Therefore, add variety to your methods using visual aids, color, music, props, etc. But, don't overdo it. Plan group activities so the trainees will talk and move around. And, be sure not to stay in one place more than a few minutes.

#74 No Performance Measurement

When asked to design and deliver a program, the trainer does just that. Afterward, it's reported everyone attended and nearly everyone liked it. The trainer's job is done.

What's Wrong?

☺ People don't learn what you want them to learn simply because they attended a class.

☺ You need to look at performance changes, not head counts.

☺ You have no way of knowing if additional learning is needed.

☺ You have no idea if you made a difference or not.

Some Success Strategies:

At the very beginning, set performance objectives. Do pre-testing and post-testing: find out what trainees know before and after your program. During the session, ask questions using active verbs such as analyze, list, compare, and contrast to determine if learning is happening. At a future time *(three weeks, three months)* ask trainees what they are doing differently since the training program. Ask their bosses what's happening that is different. Measure performance.

#75 Ignoring Evaluations

Not providing course evaluations, not reading them if they are
provided, or not learning from them will sabotage your success.

What's Wrong?

✗ You may think you have nothing more to learn.

✗ You may think you've already seen what anyone could write.

✗ You can't grow without feedback.

✗ Training programs won't improve.

✗ Attendees need a way to come to closure.

Some Success Strategies:

While you are planning the curriculum, think about the evaluation
process. Jot down sample questions that relate specifically to the
program you will teach. Once you have a list, create an evaluation
form. Use some closed questions that can be rated by numbers as well
as some open questions that ask attendees to be more specific. When
they have been collected, read all the answers; don't just scan the
numbers. Take heed and learn something!

#76 Neglecting Follow-Up

Once the curtain has fallen, trainers tend to think their job is done and neglect to do follow-up.

What's Wrong?

❑ Results are difficult to determine without follow-up.

❑ Students can forget what they learned.

❑ You move on to the next project without closure.

❑ Consultants who are trainers can lose additional business/income.

❑ Action plans are forgotten.

Some Success Strategies:

Build follow-up into the program. Make *"just checking in"* phone calls to participants from time to time. Distribute surveys a month later asking how concepts are being applied. Meet with key players to discuss action plans. Conduct a follow-up program six months later. Mail a concept reminder card to participants four weeks later. Send E-mail reminders of concepts taught in the program.

#77 Silly Screw-Ups

Putting overheads on the projector upside down, punching holes on the wrong side of the page, collating workbook pages out of order, finding the X-rated movie from the weekend in the training video box, etc. It's the little things that make a big difference.

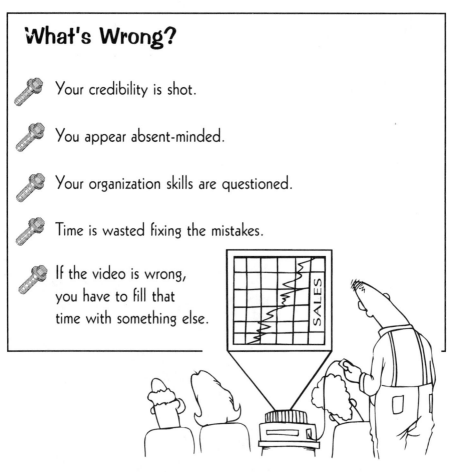

What's Wrong?

- Your credibility is shot.

- You appear absent-minded.

- Your organization skills are questioned.

- Time is wasted fixing the mistakes.

- If the video is wrong, you have to fill that time with something else.

Some Success Strategies:

Check transparencies before putting them on the projector. Go through handouts carefully before making copies. Make sure pages are lined up properly in the hole puncher. Look inside the video box before you leave your house. If all else fails, use humor and laugh at yourself. PAY ATTENTION!

Chapter 5

Media And Equipment You Depend On

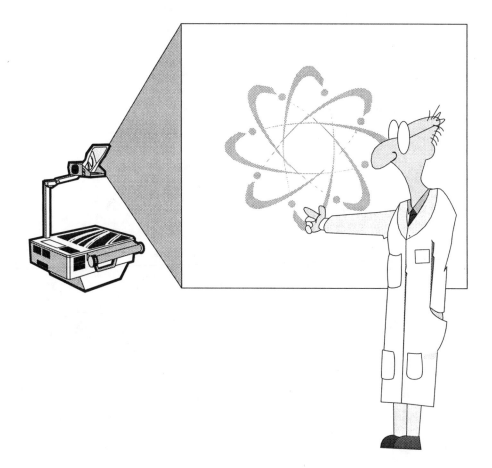

#78 Overlook Checking Equipment

Forgetting to test projectors, monitors, videocassette recorders, power sources and length of cords will cause problems.

What's Wrong?

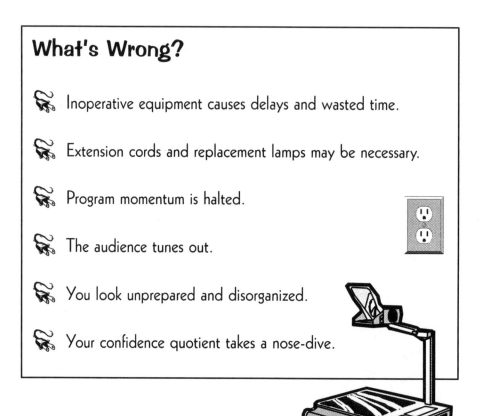

🦂 Inoperative equipment causes delays and wasted time.

🦂 Extension cords and replacement lamps may be necessary.

🦂 Program momentum is halted.

🦂 The audience tunes out.

🦂 You look unprepared and disorganized.

🦂 Your confidence quotient takes a nose-dive.

Some Success Strategies:

Arrive early and check all electrical outlets and machines that you'll be using. If equipment breaks, get replacements. In emergencies, adjust your program. Put together your personal emergency equipment kit that includes an extension cord, a spare overhead projector lamp, a video head cleaner tape and electrical tape. Use electrical tape to secure cables to the floor: this prevents you from slipping and tripping. Be prepared for anything!

#79 Visual Overload

Your fancy new workbook has pages of all colors and all kinds of charts and diagrams and cartoons and drawings and different fonts and different colors of ink...

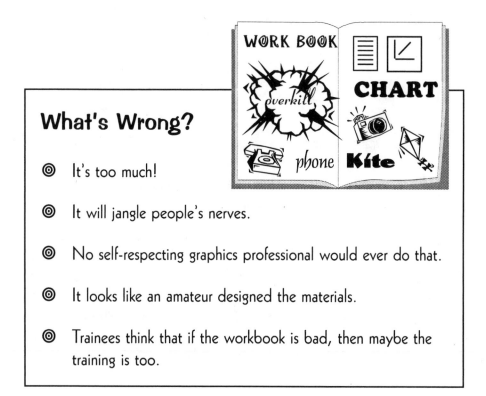

What's Wrong?

◎ It's too much!

◎ It will jangle people's nerves.

◎ No self-respecting graphics professional would ever do that.

◎ It looks like an amateur designed the materials.

◎ Trainees think that if the workbook is bad, then maybe the training is too.

Some Success Strategies:

Study good examples and follow their lead. Hire a professional graphic designer to critique your workbook. Obtain software that allows you to create classy materials. If you prefer not to learn how to create classy materials, pay someone else to do it. Remember, less is more.

#80 Forgetting To Frame

Transparencies can be framed in several ways. It takes a little longer to frame them in cardboard, but it's worth it.

What's Wrong?

☐ Naked transparencies slide around on the projector.

☐ Plastic frames with sides that turn up are messy and also tend to slide around on the projector.

☐ Sheet protector frames show punched holes and don't fill the space on top or bottom of the projector.

☐ Naked slides stick together and lead to clumsy manipulation.

☐ There's no place to write notes on naked slides.

Some Success Strategies:

Invest in cardboard frames and use them; they don't slip or slide. The white borders on cardboard frames are good for numbering or notes. Transport the framed overheads in an expandable file. Save money by reusing those without notes.

#81 Lifeless Overheads

Black-and-white, frameless, words-only transparencies are lifeless.

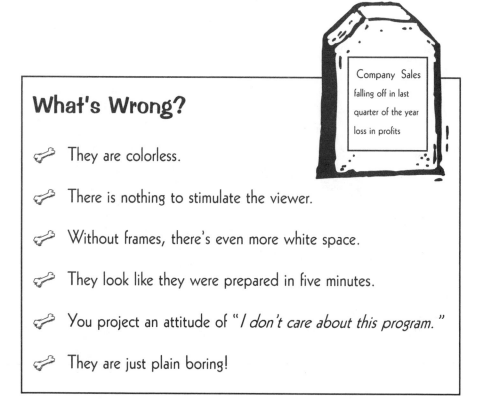

What's Wrong?

- They are colorless.

- There is nothing to stimulate the viewer.

- Without frames, there's even more white space.

- They look like they were prepared in five minutes.

- You project an attitude of "*I don't care about this program.*"

- They are just plain boring!

Company Sales falling off in last quarter of the year loss in profits

Some Success Strategies:

Use presentation software to make lively overheads. Invest in some additional clip art *(several packages are designed for business programs while others are loaded with cartoons and humorous characters)*. Plan time to develop creative overheads; use more than just words. Print them on a color *printer (if you don't have one, many fast print shops do)*. Put them in cardboard frames. If you're lazy, hire someone to make them for you, sweet-talk your coworkers, or ask your kids to help.

#82 Slideswiping

The trainer places a BIG stack of transparencies next to the projector and moves through them...reading transparency after transparency after transparency. The students feel "*slideswiped!*"

What's Wrong?

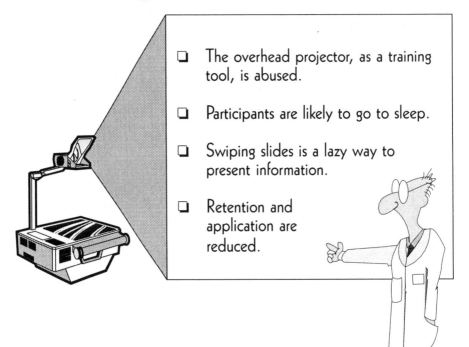

❏ The overhead projector, as a training tool, is abused.

❏ Participants are likely to go to sleep.

❏ Swiping slides is a lazy way to present information.

❏ Retention and application are reduced.

Some Success Strategies:

Remember, the overhead projector is just one of many tools available to enhance the learning process. Use transparencies only when they visually help you make your points, rather than for every point you want to make. This ensures your students don't walk away saying, "*We got slideswiped in class today!*"

#83 Blinded By The Light

Walking between the overhead projector and the screen will blind you.

What's Wrong?

🔬 You get blinded and disoriented.

🔬 Shadows block the view.

🔬 Participants get lost and confused.

🔬 You look unprofessional.

Some Success Strategies:

Have a 6' table in the front that holds your transparencies, notes, props, etc. Stand behind the table, to the right of the projector, facing the audience. Use your left hand to remove each previous overhead and place them on the left side of the projector. Use your right hand to put the next overhead in place and step back to the screen using your left hand to point things out. Don't walk between the overhead projector and the screen.

#84 Using Black Toxic Markers

The standard issue marking pens for flip charts are toxic and come in limited colors.

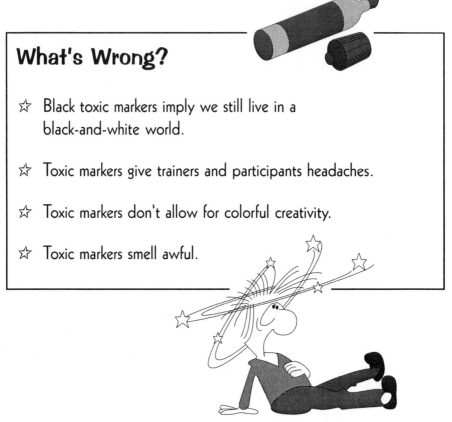

What's Wrong?

☆ Black toxic markers imply we still live in a black-and-white world.

☆ Toxic markers give trainers and participants headaches.

☆ Toxic markers don't allow for colorful creativity.

☆ Toxic markers smell awful.

Some Success Strategies:

Invest in several 12-packs of non-toxic, scented instant watercolor markers. Each color has it's own fragrance from raspberry *(magenta)* to grape *(purple)*. When you open the package, remove the black, yellow and pink markers. Use the black for name cards and the pink and yellow as highlighters. The remaining nine colors are great for flip charts. Keep a pack in your briefcase, put scented markers on your training materials check list, and stash a few packs in the training room.

#85 Marker Mishaps

You're at the flip chart, the audience is awaiting your wisdom, and your marker dried up. Maybe you forgot to put the cap on a marker and it's bleeding in your pocket. Or, you use fine point markers on the flip chart pages.

What's Wrong?

✔ Participants will chuckle as the ink bleeds in your pocket.

✔ If a marker bleeds in your pocket, your clothes are ruined.

✔ You look inept carving your writing into the flip chart, attempting to squeeze ink out of a dried-up marker.

✔ People can't read your writing when you use fine points on flip charts.

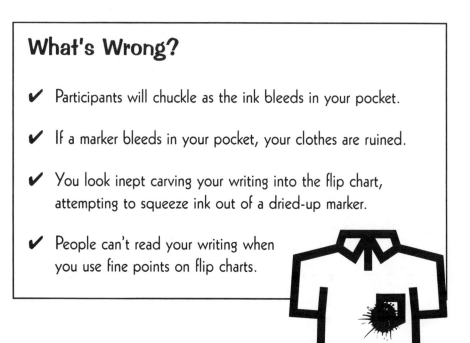

Some Success Strategies:

Test all your markers before training sessions. Be sure to have spare markers on hand for the dead or almost-dead ones. Don't put any markers in your pocket. Ever. Always tighten the caps when you're finished. Use wide tip markers for the flip chart or white board. Fine point markers are best saved for transparencies.

#86 Flopping Flip Charts

Trainers write small with a black marker on a flip chart to present all the information. They only use words. Then they flip over that page, fill up the next page with words, and then turn the page over and do it again and again and again.

What's Wrong?

✗ Once the page is flipped, the information is lost.

✗ To return to a page, you have to fumble around.

✗ The audience sees your back too much.

✗ No learning is reinforced throughout the day.

Some Success Strategies:

Remember, you don't have to fill up a whole flip chart page. It's best to write in big letters on flip charts. Draw colorful pictures and use graphs on some pages. Hang important pages on the walls, and be sure to have tape or pins that won't damage the wall coverings.

#87 Mismatched Videos

Videos used to illustrate concepts can be helpful learning tools. When the characters or situations do not match the real work world of the audience, they can be deadly. Showing a video with corporate characters and examples to a government audience is a mismatch.

What's Wrong?

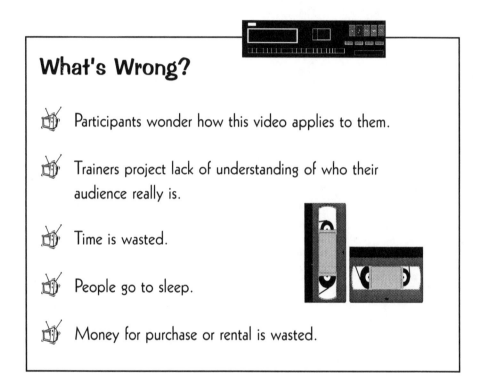

📺 Participants wonder how this video applies to them.

📺 Trainers project lack of understanding of who their audience really is.

📺 Time is wasted.

📺 People go to sleep.

📺 Money for purchase or rental is wasted.

Some Success Strategies:

During the pre-program planning phase, learn about the audience. Always preview the entire video. Be sure the situations and roles portrayed in the video match those of the audience. Don't assume participants will be able to make the connection when different roles and situations are presented.

Chapter 6

It's About Time

#88 Procrastinating

Waiting until the last minute to prepare is stressful and unnecessary.

What's Wrong?

It may be difficult to properly learn about your audience.

Course objectives and desired outcomes could be overlooked.

You won't have time to plan creative exercises, case studies, or other fun activities.

Visual aids won't be as good as they could be with careful planning.

You'll be stressed-out.

You run the risk of falling flat on your face.

Some Success Strategies:

Put reminder notes on your desk, in your organizer, on the bathroom mirror, on the dashboard of your car, etc. Tune into your mind; when you hear yourself say *"I've got plenty of time; I can do it later,"* STOP and begin it now! Ask a coworker or friend to get on your case and remind you to begin planning early.

#89 Late Starts

When you start late, for any reason, you can sabotage your success.

What's Wrong?

🕐 You send a message to participants that you don't value their time.

🕐 The audience sees you as uncaring and unprofessional.

🕐 If the room arrangement needs adjusting, you're out of luck!

🕐 Necessary flip chart pages can't be pre-pared.

🕐 You can't check equipment in advance.

🕐 There's no time to get to know the audience a little.

Some Success Strategies:

Schedule your arrival at the training site at least 45 minutes before the session is to begin. If you're going to an off-site location, call ahead to verify equipment and room arrangements are set as previously planned. Pre-prepare flip chart pages and bring the chart pad with you. To ensure that you arrive early, go to sleep early. Set your alarm 30 minutes earlier than you normally would. Check weather and traffic reports and plan accordingly.

#90 Glossing Over The Top

"On page 16 there is a diagram explaining what I just said. Next, please turn to page 17 where you will find a sample form, and on page 18 another diagram to study later. On page 19...."

What's Wrong?

➤ It wastes real teaching and learning time.

➤ The objectives aren't served using this approach.

➤ Just because they see a page doesn't mean they learn anything.

➤ Participants are overwhelmed as too much goes by too quickly.

➤ It's boring.

Some Success Strategies:

Avoid glossing over by breaking material up into smaller parts. Don't include material that is too difficult to cover. Plan your time better so you don't have to rush through material. After each concept is presented, ask participants what questions they have and watch the time you spend answering them. Stimulate discussion by asking questions, putting people in groups, etc.

#91 Bad Breaks

Poor break management means breaks are too long, too short, too many, too few, or that a specific break schedule must be followed.

What's Wrong?

Lengthy breaks waste training time and you lose momentum.

Short breaks frustrate those in the food and bathroom lines.

With too many breaks, trainees get the impression you're just filling time.

Too few breaks don't allow participants to stretch and move around and stay sharp.

Some Success Strategies:

Plan structured breaks (10-15 minutes) into the course outline, but allow yourself some flexibility. Avoid an attitude of *"I have to stick to my outline, no matter what."* When trainees are squirming and looking at their watches, it's time for a short break. To avoid stopping in the middle of important content for a structured break, take a quick one-minute stretch break until you can break longer.

#92 Running Out Of Time

The session is flowing nicely and suddenly you realize you have thirty minutes of material to cover and only ten minutes left. You either keep going and stop late, or stop, unfinished, on time.

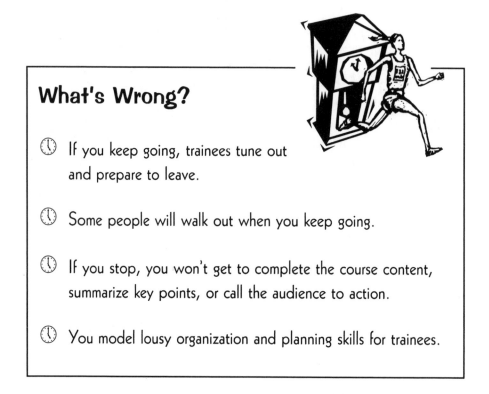

What's Wrong?

🕐 If you keep going, trainees tune out and prepare to leave.

🕐 Some people will walk out when you keep going.

🕐 If you stop, you won't get to complete the course content, summarize key points, or call the audience to action.

🕐 You model lousy organization and planning skills for trainees.

Some Success Strategies:

Prepare an accurate timetable in advance, and stick to it. Plan flexible time into the schedule in case you need it. Identify what you can leave out if you're running slow. Know how you can expand your material if you're running ahead of time. At breaks and other opportunities, review your schedule and make timing adjustments.

Chapter 7

Other Stupid Stuff

#93 Snooze Foods

Snooze foods include anything that can put the audience to sleep.

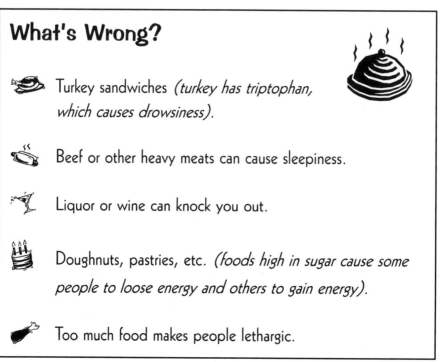

What's Wrong?

Turkey sandwiches *(turkey has triptophan, which causes drowsiness).*

Beef or other heavy meats can cause sleepiness.

Liquor or wine can knock you out.

Doughnuts, pastries, etc. *(foods high in sugar cause some people to loose energy and others to gain energy).*

Too much food makes people lethargic.

Some Success Strategies:

For breakfast serve fruits, cereal, yogurt, sugarfree muffins, and bagels. For lunch serve salads, fruit, broiled chicken, etc. For afternoon snacks serve fruit, yogurt, low-fat granola bars, etc.
Always have plenty of water and juice around throughout the day.
Remember to plan the meals as you would plan the program. If in doubt about what to serve, consult a food expert. And, don't let the laxatives get mixed in with the chocolate mints!

#94 Double-Booking Yourself

"I'll be in Cleveland for training that morning, so I'll be able to speak at the luncheon downtown and then get over to the airport hotel in time to train the new group in the afternoon; and then I'll catch the 7 P.M. flight home."

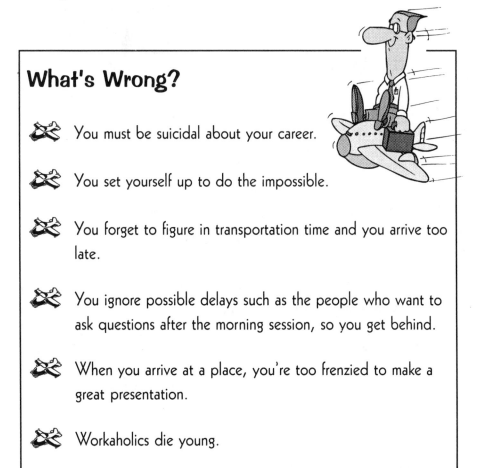

What's Wrong?

- You must be suicidal about your career.

- You set yourself up to do the impossible.

- You forget to figure in transportation time and you arrive too late.

- You ignore possible delays such as the people who want to ask questions after the morning session, so you get behind.

- When you arrive at a place, you're too frenzied to make a great presentation.

- Workaholics die young.

Some Success Strategies:

Learn to say *"no"* and to negotiate. Pass the additional engagements to a colleague or coworker. Make it a priority to keep balance in your life.

#95 Too Tight Shoes

Your laces are tied too tight or your shoes don't fit right.

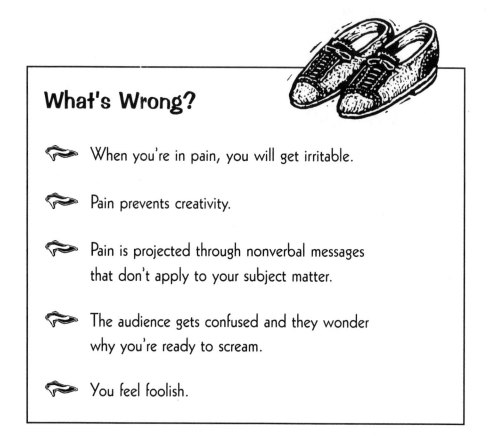

What's Wrong?

🤚 When you're in pain, you will get irritable.

🤚 Pain prevents creativity.

🤚 Pain is projected through nonverbal messages
that don't apply to your subject matter.

🤚 The audience gets confused and they wonder
why you're ready to scream.

🤚 You feel foolish.

Some Success Strategies:

Break in new shoes long before their classroom debut. Stop for a
minute and loosen your laces. When your shoes are too tight and
you'd be more comfortable without them, create a spontaneous exercise where participants need to take off their shoes, too. Or, keep a
spare pair of comfortable shoes to put on.

#96 Assuming They Care

You may be passionate about your topic and you love to share that passion. They may not care about the topic at all, or worse, about being in a room with you to listen to it.

What's Wrong?

☹ Assumptions leave you open to surprises and disappointments.

☹ Some people may think they know it all by now.

☹ Some people may be indifferent to your favorite subject.

☹ Several may be *"hostages"* who are mandated to attend.

☹ Conflicting agendas cause frustration and anxiety.

Some Success Strategies:

Never make assumptions about anything! In the pre-program preparation phase, find out as much as you can about participants' knowledge level and interests. During the program, after you have delivered your *"grab the audience"* beginning, qualify them. Ask questions about their background and enthusiasm level regarding the topic. Be prepared to *"sell"* your topic to uninterested people. Provide benefit statements for your audience and move on.

#97 Losing Your Place

When you use a set of pages as your instructor guides *(notes)* and you get lost, your pages can fall on the floor. Then you have to crawl around on the floor like a baby.

What's Wrong?

- 📖 Trainees begin to doubt your organizing ability.

- 📖 There's a good chance you will lose credibility.

- 📖 This may be a clue you are not following your outline.

- 📖 You look like you don't care, so trainees can decide not to care too.

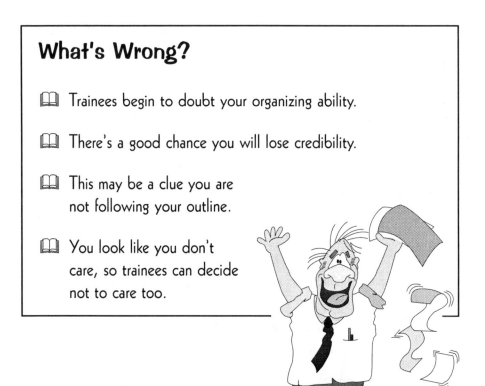

Some Success Strategies:

There is no reason to keep a secret about keeping your place in your notes. Use a marker, a pencil, a small ruler, or even a small toy to keep track of where you are as you proceed through your notes. Be sure your notes are securely bound in a loose-leaf notebook, or with staples.

#98 Using Collapsible Pointers

Generally, pointers can be troublesome, but those collapsible ones can be deadly.

What's Wrong:

♦ Trainers tend to play with them, which is very distracting.

♦ They inhibit nonverbal communication.

♦ They're cumbersome.

♦ They're lethal.

♦ One trainer tried to collapse one on his hip, but instead it slid into his stomach...ouch!

Some Success Strategies:

In a classroom, step back to the screen, face the audience, and use your hand to point to the screen. If you must use a pointer, use a solid one and put it down immediately after you've pointed. Be careful with laser pointers; practice a lot to avoid a dancing arrow pointing to everything but your screen!

#99 Hot Microphone

Forgetting to turn off your wireless microphone when you visit the restroom is every trainer's nightmare. We all probably know someone who has done it.

What's Wrong?

The audience knows where you've been.

They've heard everything!

You're horribly embarrassed.

It's hard to stay focused and continue the program.

Some Success Strategies:

If you're in a room that requires you to wear a wireless microphone, then turn it off as soon as you stop to take a break. Better yet, take it off: there's always a chance you could inadvertently turn it back on. If you still forget, use humor to bail yourself out. You could say, *"Well, now that I've got your attention, let's get started again."*

#100 Forgetting Your Glasses

You're in such a hurry to leave that you forget and leave your glasses in the house, the hotel, or the car.

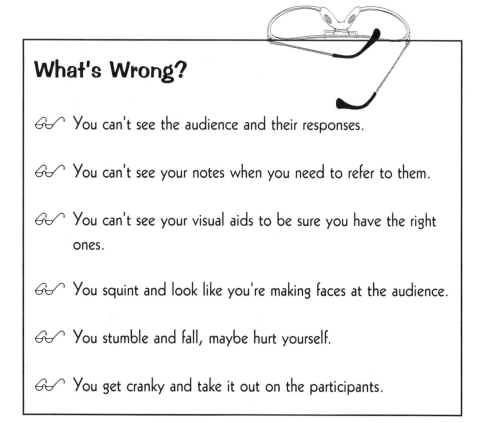

What's Wrong?

&~ You can't see the audience and their responses.

&~ You can't see your notes when you need to refer to them.

&~ You can't see your visual aids to be sure you have the right ones.

&~ You squint and look like you're making faces at the audience.

&~ You stumble and fall, maybe hurt yourself.

&~ You get cranky and take it out on the participants.

Some Success Strategies:

Keep a spare pair of glasses with you at all times. If possible, borrow glasses from someone in the audience who has a similar prescription. Wear contact lenses. Have corrective eye surgery so you don't need glasses to forget. Lastly, make a joke about it.

#101 Lost Luggage

It's evening. You arrive in Dallas and your luggage arrives in Cleveland. Your training program is in the morning.

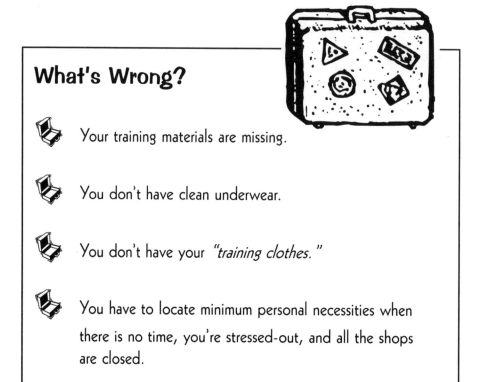

What's Wrong?

Your training materials are missing.

You don't have clean underwear.

You don't have your *"training clothes."*

You have to locate minimum personal necessities when there is no time, you're stressed-out, and all the shops are closed.

Some Success Strategies:

Carry on to the plane your training materials as well as a change of underwear, toothbrush and other small personal essentials. Travel wearing something that would be appropriate for your training session just in case you have to wear it again. Be prepared to tell the old story about the trainer you knew who went to Dallas, but the luggage went to Cleveland....

Summary

"Stupid things you do can sabotage your success."

Stern & Payment

Before developing or delivering a training program, take a few minutes to review a few of the stupid things described in this book. Remember, *"stupid"* is about what we do, not who we are. Stupid comes from a Latin word meaning senseless and dull. *(Definitely not you or your work!)*

To prepare to become the best you can be, think about different aspects of the place where your training program will occur. Is it inside or outside, light or dark, cramped or oversized, etc.?

Consider the best ways to look and act. For your program, is it best to have casual or formal dress and demeanor? What can you do in advance to pave the way for success?

Prepare what you plan to say and how you will say it. Flexibility is in and total impromptu is out. Build in your own personal warning signs and reminders to stop, look, listen, and honor your audience.

Carefully select the methods, media, materials and equipment you will use. Today everyone expects information and learning to be wrapped in some glitz and razzle-dazzle. Plan ahead for what is most appropriate in your training situation.

Familiarity with the *"stupid things"* in this book will help you avoid collecting a large personal supply of embarrassing moments and other *"stupid stuff."*

Focus on the success strategies. Think of ways you can apply them to improve your training every time, one small step at a time.

WANTED:

More Stupid Things

Did we overlook your favorite stupid thing? We'd appreciate hearing about it so we can share it with your colleagues. Tell us about it on this form, or make copies. Send more stupid things trainers do to sabotage success to:

> Stern & Payment
> 515 Stratford Court
> Del Mar, CA 92014-2722
> Fax: 619-792-2745

MY FAVORITE STUPID THING IS:
(describe and elaborate)

OPTIONAL:

Name:_____

Organization:_____

Address:_____

Phone:_____   Fax: _____

About The Publisher

Richard Chang Associates, Inc. is a diversified organizational improvement consulting firm based in Irvine, California. They provide a wide range of products and services to organizations worldwide in the areas of organizational development, quality improvement, team performance, and learning systems. The Publications Division of Richard Chang Associates, Inc., established to provide individuals with a wide variety of practical resources for continuous learning in the workplace or on a personal level, is pleased to bring you this book.

RICHARD CHANG ASSOCIATES

Richard Chang Associates, Inc.
Publications Division
15265 Alton Parkway, Suite 300
Irvine, CA 92618
(800) 756-8096 Fax (714) 727-7007

ADDITIONAL RESOURCES
FROM RICHARD CHANG ASSOCIATES, INC.
PUBLICATIONS DIVISION

PRACTICAL GUIDEBOOK COLLECTION

QUALITY IMPROVEMENT SERIES

Continuous Process Improvement

Continuous Improvement Tools, Volume 1

Continuous Improvement Tools, Volume 2

Step-By-Step Problem Solving

Meetings That Work!

Improving Through Benchmarking

Succeeding As A Self-Managed Team

Satisfying Internal Customers First!

Process Reengineering In Action

Measuring Organizational Improvement Impact

MANAGEMENT SKILLS SERIES

Coaching Through Effective Feedback

Expanding Leadership Impact

Mastering Change Management

On-The-Job Orientation And Training

Re-Creating Teams During Transitions

Planning Successful Employee Performance

Coaching For Peak Employee Performance

Evaluating Employee Performance

Interviewing And Selecting High Performers

HIGH-IMPACT TRAINING SERIES

Creating High-Impact Training

Identifying Targeted Training Needs

Mapping A Winning Training Approach

Producing High-Impact Learning Tools

Applying Successful Training Techniques

Measuring The Impact Of Training

Make Your Training Results Last

WORKPLACE DIVERSITY SERIES

Capitalizing On Workplace Diversity

Successful Staffing In A Diverse Workplace

Team Building For Diverse Work Groups

Communicating In A Diverse Workplace

Tools For Valuing Diversity

HIGH PERFORMANCE TEAM SERIES

Success Through Teamwork

Building A Dynamic Team

Measuring Team Performance

Team Decision-Making Techniques

Guidebooks are also available in fine bookstores.

ADDITIONAL RESOURCES
FROM RICHARD CHANG ASSOCIATES, INC.
PUBLICATIONS DIVISION

PERSONAL GROWTH AND DEVELOPMENT COLLECTION
Managing Your Career in a Changing Workplace
Unlocking Your Career Potential
Marketing Yourself and Your Career
Making Career Transitions

101 STUPID THINGS SERIES
101 Stupid Things Trainers Do To Sabotage Success
101 Stupid Things Supervisors Do To Sabotage Success
101 Stupid Things Salespeople Do To Sabotage Success
101 Stupid Things Business Travelers Do To Sabotage Success
101 Stupid Things Employees Do To Sabotage Success

TRAINING PRODUCTS
Step-By-Step Problem Solving TOOLKIT™
Meetings That Work! Practical Guidebook TOOLPAK™
Continuous Improvement Tools Volume 1 Practical Guidebook TOOLPAK™

PACKAGED TRAINING PROGRAMS
High Involvement Teamwork™
Continuous Process Improvement

VIDEOTAPES
Mastering Change Management**
Quality: You Don't Have To Be Sick To Get Better*
Achieving Results Through Quality Improvement*
Total Quality: Myths, Methods, Or Miracles**
　　Featuring Drs. Ken Blanchard and Richard Chang
Empowering The Quality Effort**
　　Featuring Drs. Ken Blanchard and Richard Chang
Optimizing Customer Value*
　　Featuring Richard Chang
Creating High-Impact Training*
　　Featuring Richard Chang

TOTAL QUALITY VIDEO SERIES AND WORKBOOKS
Building Commitment**
Teaming Up**
Applied Problem Solving**
Self-Directed Evaluation**

* Produced by American Media Inc.　　** Produced by Double Vision Studios